Oakland Athletics 2019

A Baseball Companion

Edited by Patrick Dubuque, Aaron Gleeman and Bret Sayre

Baseball Prospectus

Craig Brown and Dave Pease, Consultant Editors
Rob McQuown and Harry Pavlidis, Statistics Editors

Copyright © 2019 by DIY Baseball, LLC.
All rights reserved

This book or any part thereof may not be reproduced or transmitted in any form or by any means, electronic or mechanical, including photocopying, recording, or by any information storage and retrieval system, without permission in writing from the publisher.

Limit of Liability/Disclaimer of Warranty: While the publisher and the author have used their best efforts in preparing this book, they make no representations or warranties with respect to the accuracy or completeness of the contents of this book and specifically disclaim any implied warranties of merchantability or fitness for a particular purpose. No warranty may be created or extended by sales representatives or written sales materials. The advice and strategies contained herein may not be suitable for your situation. You should consult with a professional where appropriate. Neither the publisher nor the author shall be liable for any loss of profit or any other commercial damages, including but not limited to special, incidental, consequential, or other damages.

Library of Congress Cataloging-in-Publication Data:
paperback
ISBN-13: 978-1-949332-20-9

Project Credits
Cover Design: Kathleen Dyson
Interior Design and Production: Jeff Pease, Dave Pease
Layout: Jeff Pease, Dave Pease

Baseball icon courtesy of Uberux, from https://www.shareicon.net/author/uberux

Ballpark diagram courtesy of Lou Spirito/THIRTY81 Project, https://thirty81project.com/

Manufactured in the United States of America
10 9 8 7 6 5 4 3 2 1

Table of Contents

Foreword v
    Rob Mains

Statistical Introduction vii

Part 1: Team Analysis

Table for Two: Previewing the 2019 Oakland Athletics 3
    Jon Hegglund and Bret Sayre

Performance Graphs 7

2018 Team Performance 8

2019 Team Projections 9

Team Personnel 10

Oakland–Alameda County Coliseum Stats 11

Athletics Team Analysis 13

Part 2: Player Analysis

Athletics Player Analysis 20

Athletics Prospects 91

Part 3: Featured Articles

The Hole in The Shift is Fixing Itself 105
    Russell Carleton

The State of the Quality Start 109
    Rob Mains

Heads-Up Hacking—The First Pitch 115
    Matthew Trueblood

A Hymn for the Index Stat 121
    Patrick Dubuque

Index of Names 125

Foreword

Rob Mains

Welcome to this companion of the 2019 Oakland Athletics. We at Baseball Prospectus are excited to provide this analysis of the Athletics.

Our website, Baseball Prospectus, is a leader in delivering high-quality commentary and data to baseball fans everywhere. To some, those words—commentary and data—appear mutually exclusive. There are people out there who believe that traditional analysis and advanced analytics must run on different paths. But the simplistic narrative of stats vs. traditionalists just isn't true. Every team's analytics department interacts with scouting, development, and major league operations with a common goal: Delivering a championship. New technologies, like radar tracking of pitch speeds and movement, enable talent evaluators to focus on qualitative aspects of pitching like mechanics and pitch sequencing. In-game strategies like infield shifts, based on batters' hit tendencies, help turn balls in play into outs. Hitters use information to adjust their swings to maximize run production.

All these numbers can seem, at best, intimidating, and at worst, counterproductive to the casual fan. Even as technology and analysis have embedded themselves deeply into the way teams run, it can often feel like statistics create a displacement between the viewer and the sport, breaking them out of the action. And yet every fan incorporates the numbers to some degree; stats like batting average and earned run average, so fundamental to how we talk about performance, are actually complicated formulas. They don't bother people because those formulas have become second nature, as easy to translate as the action on the field.

Along the way, new statistics have entered baseball's lexicon. You'll see some of them, like on-base percentage (which measures a batter's ability to get on base via walk, hit batter, or hit), OPS (on-base plus slugging), and average exit velocity (the speed of balls off a hitter's bat) on broadcasts. Others, like DRC+, might well be new to you. Some of them have been well-defined to the public, others haven't. That lack of context has created ambiguity. Fans know that a ball hit 100 mph is scorched, but does that mean extra bases? (Not if it's hit on the ground or high in the air it doesn't.)

For those who are amenable to them, the new statistics can increase the enjoyment and understanding of the game. They can help fans identify when a pitcher is tiring, when a stolen base or a bunt attempt makes sense (and, more often, when it doesn't), or how a team's lineup might be constructed. Websites like Baseball Prospectus add to that understanding by weaving metrics into the narrative of the game. That's the goal of this publication: to take some of the newer, more complicated statistics and make them as intuitive as the ones on the back of old baseball cards.

But you don't need to love analytics to love baseball. The fans at BP who worked together to write this guide are captivated first and foremost by the game itself. We're drawn to Aaron Judge's power, Francisco Lindor's glove, Billy Hamilton's speed and Patrick Corbin's slider and don't need numbers to tell us why they're so mesmerizing. The underlying statistics provide depth to the game that we all love.

We hope you'll find that this guide helps you better understand the Athletics. Our analysts have studied the team's major league personnel and its minor league affiliates to identify their strengths and weaknesses, both the obvious ones and those that only a careful dissection of players' performances—yes, including the data—can reveal. You don't need us to tell you who was good and who wasn't in 2018, but our models and writers can help you project how each player is going to perform this year and beyond, and appreciate the greatness of each new game as it unfolds. As in the sport itself, the human and analytic components combine to generate a deeper overall understanding.

Think back to the first time you saw a baseball game on a high-definition TV. You'd grown familiar with how the game looked and felt on a picture tube. But new TV allowed you to see details that you'd never seen before. That's how advanced statistics work. The game itself is why you're here and why you're buying this. (And, for that matter, why we wrote it.) The statistical measures provide the sharper focus, the detail, the depth of knowledge that you didn't have before, generating an overall superior picture. Enjoy the view.

—Rob Mains is an author of Baseball Prospectus.

Statistical Introduction

Sports are, fundamentally, a blend of athletic endeavor and storytelling. Baseball, like any other sport, tells its stories in so many ways: in the arc of a game from the stands or a season from the box scores, in photos, or even in numbers. At Baseball Prospectus, we understand that statistics don't replace observation or any of baseball's stories, but complement everything else that makes the game so much fun.

What stats help us with is with patterns and precision, variance and value. This book can help you learn things you may not see from watching a game or hundred, whether it's the path of a career over time or the breadth of the entire MLB. We'd also never ask you to choose between our numbers and the experience of viewing a game from the cheap seats or the comfort of your home; our publication combines running the numbers with observations and wisdom from some of the brightest minds we can find. But if you *do* want to learn more about the numbers beyond what's on the backs of player jerseys, let us help explain.

Offense

At the end of this past year, we've revised our methodology for determining batting value. Long-time readers of Baseball Prospectus will notice that we've retired True Average in favor of a new metric: Deserved Runs Created Plus (DRC+). Developed by Jonathan Judge and our stats team, this statistic measures everything a player does at the plate–reaching base, hitting for power, making outs, and moving runners over–and puts it on a scale where 100 equals league-average performance. A DRC+ of 150 is terrific, a DRC+ of 100 is average, and a DRC+ of 75 means you better be an excellent defender.

DRC+ also does a better job than any of our previous metrics in taking contextual factors into account. The model adjusts for how the park affects performance, but also for things like the talent of the opposing pitcher, value of different types of batted-ball events, league, temperature, and other factors. It's able to describe a player's expected offensive contribution than any other statistic we've found over the years, and also does a better job of predicting future performance as well.

The other aspect of run-scoring is baserunning, which we quantify using Baserunning Runs. BRR not only records the value of stolen bases (or getting caught in the act), but also accounts for a runner's ability to go first to third on a single or advance on a fly ball.

Defense

Where offensive value is *relatively* easy to identify and understand, defensive value is … not. Over the past dozen years, the sabermetric community has focused mostly on stats based on zone data: a real-live human person records the type of batted ball and estimated landing location, and models are created that give expected outs. From there, you can compare fielders' actual outs to those expected ones. Simple, right?

Unfortunately, zone data has two major issues. First, zone data is recorded by commercial data providers who keep the raw data private unless you pay for it. (All the statistics we build in this book and on our website use public data as inputs.) That hurts our ability to test assumptions or duplicate results. Second, over the years it has become apparent that there's quite a bit of "noise" in zone-based fielding analysis. Sometimes the conclusions drawn from zone data don't hold up to scrutiny, and sometimes the different data provided by different providers don't look anything alike, giving wildly different results. Sometimes the hard-working professional stringers or scorers might unknowingly inflict unconscious bias into the mix: for example good fielders will often be credited with more expected outs despite the data, and ballparks with high press boxes tend to score more line drives than ones with a lower press box.

Enter our Fielding Runs Above Average (FRAA). For most positions, FRAA is built from play-by-play data, which allows us to avoid the subjectivity found in many other fielding metrics. The idea is this: count how many fielding plays are made by a given player and compare that to expected plays for an average fielder at their position (based on pitcher ground-ball tendencies and batter handedness). Then we adjust for park and base-out situations.

When it comes to catchers, our methodology is a little different thanks to the laundry list of responsibilities they're tasked with beyond just, well, catching and throwing the ball. By now you've probably heard about "framing" or the art of making umpires more likely to call balls outside the strike zone for strikes. To put this into one tidy number, we incorporate pitch tracking data (for the years it exists) and adjust for important factors like pitcher, umpire, batter, and home-field advantage using a mixed-model approach. This grants us a number for how many strikes the catcher is personally adding to (or subtracting from) his pitchers' performance … which we then convert to runs added or lost using linear weights.

Framing is one of the biggest parts of determining catcher value, but we also take into account blocking balls from going past, whether a scorer deems it a passed ball or a wild pitch. We use a similar approach–one that really benefits from the pitch tracking data that tells us what ends up in the dirt and what doesn't. We also include a catcher's ability to prevent stolen bases and how well they field balls in play, and *finally* we come up with our FRAA for catchers.

Pitching

Both pitching and fielding make up the half of baseball that isn't run scoring: run prevention. Separating pitching from fielding is a tough task, and most recent pitching analysis has branched off from Voros McCracken's famous (and controversial) statement, "There is little if any difference among major-league pitchers in their ability to prevent hits on balls hit in the field of play." The research of the analytic community has validated this to some extent, and there are a host of "defense-independent" pitching measures that have been developed to try and extricate the effect of the defense behind a hurler from the pitcher's work.

Our solution to this quandry is Deserved Run Average (DRA), our core pitching metric. DRA looks like earned run average (ERA), the tried-and-true pitching stat you've seen on every baseball broadcast or box score from the past century, but it's very different. To start, DRA takes an event-by-event look at what the pitchers does, and adjusts the value of that event based on different environmental factors like park, batter, catcher, umpire, base-out situation, run differential, inning, defense, home field advantage, pitcher role, and temperature. That mixed model gives us a pitcher's expected contribution, similar to what we do for our DRC+ model for hitters and FRAA model for catchers. (Oh, and we also consider the pitcher's effect on basestealing and on balls getting past the catcher.)

It's important to note that DRA is set to the scale of runs allowed per nine innings (RA9) instead of ERA, which makes DRA's scale slightly higher than ERA's. The reason for this is because ERA tends to overrate three types of pitchers:

1. Pitchers who play in parks where scorers hand out more errors. Official scorers differ significantly in the frequency at which they assign errors to fielders.
2. Ground-ball pitchers, because a substantial proportion of errors occur on grounders.
3. Pitchers who aren't very good. Better pitchers often allow fewer unearned runs than bad pitchers, because good pitchers tend to find ways to get out of jams.

Since the last time you picked up an edition of this book, we've also made a few minor changes to DRA to make it better. Recent research into "tunneling"–the act of throwing consecutive pitches that appear similar from a batter's point of view until after the swing decision point–data has given us a new contextual factor to account for in DRA: plate distance. This refers to the distance between successive pitches as they approach the plate, and while it has a smaller effect than factors like velocity or whiff rate, it still can help explain pitcher strikeout rate in our model.

New Pitching Metrics for 2019

We're including a few "new" pitching metrics for 2019's suite of Baseball Prospectus publications, but you may be familiar with them if you've spent time scouring the internet for stats.

Fastball Percentage

Our fastball percentage (FB%) statistic measures how frequently a pitcher throws a pitch classified as a "fastball," measured as a percentage of overall pitches thrown. We qualify three types of fastballs:

1. The traditional four-seam fastball;
2. The two-seam fastball or sinker;
3. "Hard cutters," which are pitches that have the movement profile of a cut fastball and are used as the pitcher's primary offering or in place of a more traditional fastball.

For example, a pitcher with a FB% of 67 throws any combination of these three pitches about two-thirds of the time.

Whiff Rate

Everybody loves a swing and a miss, and whiff rate (WHF) measures how frequently pitchers induce a swinging strike. To calculate WHF, we add up all the pitches thrown that ended with a swinging strike, then divide that number by a pitcher's total pitches thrown. Most often, high whiff rates correlate with high strikeout rates (and overall effective pitcher performance).

Called Strike Probability

Called Strike Probability (CSP) is a number that represents the likelihood that all of a pitcher's pitches will be called a strike while controlling for location, pitcher and batter handedness, umpire and count. Here's how it works: on each pitch, our model determines how many times (out of 100) that a similar pitch was called for a strike given those factors mentioned above, and when normalized for each batter's strike zone. Then we average the CSP for all pitches thrown by a pitcher in a season, and that gives us the yearly CSP percentage you see in the stats boxes.

As you might imagine, pitchers with a higher CSP are more likely to work in the zone, where pitchers with a lower CSP are likely locating their pitches outside the normal strike zone, for better or for worse.

Projections

Many of you aren't turning to this book just for a look at what a player has done, but for a look at what a player is going to do: the PECOTA projections. PECOTA, initially developed by Nate Silver (who has moved on to greater fame as a political analyst), consists of three parts:

1. Major-league equivalencies, which use minor-league statistics to project how a player will perform in the major leagues;
2. Baseline forecasts, which use weighted averages and regression to the mean to estimate a player's current true talent level; and
3. Aging curves, which uses the career paths of comparable players to estimate how a player's statistics are likely to change over time.

With all those important things covered, let's take a look at what's in the book this year.

Team Prospectus

You bought this book to learn more about your favorite (or maybe least-favorite, who are we to judge?) team, so let's talk about them. After a thoughtful preview of the 2019 season, you'll be presented with our Team Prospectus. This outlines many of the key statistics for each team's 2018 season, as well as a very inviting stadium diagram.

First you'll find the Performance Graphs page. The first is the 2018 Hit List Ranking. This shows our Hit List Rank for the team on each day of the 2018 season and is intended to give you a picture of the ups and downs of the team's season, including their highest and lowest ranks of the year. Hit List Rank measures overall team performance and drives the Hit List Power Rankings at the baseballprospectus.com website.

The second graph is Committed Payroll and helps you see how the team's payroll has compared to the MLB and divisional average payrolls over time. Payroll figures are currents as of January 1, 2019; with so many free agents still unsigned as of this writing, the final 2018 figure will likely be significantly different for many teams. (In the meantime, you can always find the most current data at Baseball Prospectus' Cot's Baseball Contracts page.)

Oakland Athletics 2019

The third graph is Farm System Ranking and displays how the Baseball Prospectus prospect team has ranked the organization's farm system since 2007. It also indicates the highest and lowest ranks that the farm system achieved over that time.

We start the Team Performance page with the squad's unadjusted and third-order 2018 win-loss records, presented in divisional context. We then list the three highest performing hitters and pitchers by WARP for 2018. Beneath that are a host of other team statistics. **Pythag** presents an adjusted 2018 winning percentage, calculated by taking runs scored per game (**RS/G**) and runs allowed per game (**RA/G**) for the team, and running them through a version of Bill James' Pythagorean formula that was refined and improved by David Smyth and Brandon Heipp. (The formula is called "Pythagenpat," which is equally fun to type and to say.)

Next up is **DRC+**, described earlier, to indicate the overall hitting ability of the team either above or below league-average. Run prevention on the pitching side is covered by **DRA** (also mentioned earlier) and another metric: Fielding Independent Pitching (**FIP**), which calculates another ERA-like statistic based on strikeouts, walks, and home runs recorded. Defensive Efficiency Rating (**DER**) tells us the percentage of balls in play turned into outs for the team, and is a quick fielding shorthand that rounds out run prevention.

After that, we have several measures related to roster composition, as opposed to on-field performance. **B-Age** and **P-Age** tell us the average age of a team's batters and pitchers, respectively. **Salary** is the combined team payroll for all on-field players, and Doug Pappas' Marginal Dollars per Marginal Win (**M$/MW**) tells us how much money a team spent to earn production above replacement level.

Ending this batch of statistics is the number of disabled list days a team had over the season (**DL Days**) and the amount of salary paid to players on the disabled list (**$ on DL**); this final number is expressed as a percentage of total payroll.

Next to each of these stats, we've listed each team's MLB rank in that category from 1st to 30th. In this, 1st always indicates a positive outcome and 30th a negative outcome, except in the case of salary–1st is highest.

The Team Projections page is intended to convey the team's operational capacity entering the 2019 season. We start with the team's PECOTA projected record for 2019, again in divisional context. The **+/-** column indicates how many more or less wins the team is projected to get than they got in 2018. We then list the three highest projected hitters and pitchers by WARP for 2018. A brief farm system summary follows, with the team's top prospect and number of BP Top 101 Prospects. Finally, we list the key new players and departed players, along with their 2019 projected WARP.

Alex Bregman 3B

Born: 03/30/94 Age: 25 Bats: R Throws: R
Height: 6'0" Weight: 180 Origin: Round 1, 2015 Draft (#2 overall)

YEAR	TEAM	LVL	AGE	PA	R	2B	3B	HR	RBI	BB	K	SB	CS	AVG/OBP/SLG
2016	CCH	AA	22	285	54	16	2	14	46	42	26	5	3	.297/.415/.559
2016	FRE	AAA	22	83	17	6	0	6	15	5	12	2	1	.333/.373/.641
2016	HOU	MLB	22	217	31	13	3	8	34	15	52	2	0	.264/.313/.478
2017	HOU	MLB	23	626	88	39	5	19	71	55	97	17	5	.284/.352/.475
2018	HOU	MLB	24	705	105	51	1	31	103	96	85	10	4	.286/.394/.532
2019	HOU	MLB	25	675	96	38	3	23	78	73	107	12	4	.272/.359/.463

Breakout: 6% Improve: 52% Collapse: 5% Attrition: 2% MLB: 100%
Comparables: Anthony Rendon, David Wright, Pablo Sandoval

YEAR	TEAM	LVL	AGE	PA	DRC+	VORP	BABIP	BRR	FRAA	WARP
2016	CCH	AA	22	285	172	38.9	.286	1.6	SS(51): -3.4, 3B(11): 1.4	2.7
2016	FRE	AAA	22	83	161	10.0	.333	-1.2	SS(14): 2.1, LF(3): -0.1	0.8
2016	HOU	MLB	22	217	107	9.6	.317	0.5	3B(40): 0.9, SS(6): -0.1	1.1
2017	HOU	MLB	23	626	114	34.7	.311	-1.5	3B(132): 8.7, SS(30): -2.9	3.9
2018	HOU	MLB	24	705	150	72.6	.289	-1.6	3B(136): 5.4, SS(28): -0.4	7.4
2019	HOU	MLB	25	675	125	37.3	.295	0.0	3B 7, SS 0	4.6

After the projections page, we share a few items about the team's home ballpark. There's the aforementioned diagram of the park's dimensions (including distances to the outfield wall), a few important biographical facts about the stadium, a graphic showing the height of the wall from the left-field pole to the right-field pole, and a table showing three-year park factors for the stadium. The park factors are displayed as indexes where 100 is average, 110 means that the park inflates the statistic in question by 10 percent, and 90 means that the park deflates the statistic in question by 10 percent.

Following the ballpark page, we have a **Personnel** section that lists many of the important decision-makers and upper-level field and operations staff members for the franchise, as well as any former Baseball Prospectus staff members who are currently part of the organization.

Position Players

After all that information and a thoughtful bylined essay covering each team, we present our player comments. Each player is listed with the major-league team who employed him as of early January 2019. If a player changed teams after that point via free agency, trade, or any other method, you'll be able to find them in the book for their previous squad.

First, we cover biographical information (age is as of June 30, 2019) before moving onto the stats themselves. Our statistic columns include standard identifying information like **YEAR**, **TEAM**, **LVL** (level of affiliated play) and **AGE** before getting into the numbers. Next, we provide raw, unstranslated numbers like you might find on the back of your dad's baseball cards: **PA** (plate appearances), **R** (runs), **2B** (doubles), **3B** (triples), **HR** (home runs), **RBI** (runs batted in), **BB** (walks), **K** (strikeouts), **SB** (stolen bases) and **CS** (caught stealing). Then we have unadjusted "slash" statistics: **AVG** (batting average), **OBP** (on-base percentage) and **SLG** (slugging percentage).

Just below the stats box is **PECOTA** data, which is discussed further in a following section. After that, it's on to a pithy and always-informative comment written by a member of the Baseball Prospectus staff, before we cover more stats.

The second text box repeats YEAR, TEAM, LVL, AGE, and PA, then moves on to **DRC+** (Deserved Runs Created Plus), which we described earlier as total offensive expected contribution compared to the league average. Next, one of our oldest active metrics, **VORP** (Value Over Replacement Player), considers offensive production, position and plate appearances. In essence, it is the number of runs contributed beyond what a replacement-level player at the same position would contribute if given the same percentage of team plate appearances. VORP does not consider the quality of a player's defense.

BABIP (batting average on balls in play) tells us how often a ball in play fell for a hit, and can help us identify whether a batter may have been lucky or not … but note that high BABIPs also tend to follow the great hitters of our time, as well as speedy singles hitters who put the ball on the ground.

The next item is **BRR** (Baserunning Runs), which covers all of a player's baserunning accomplishments which includes (but isn't limited to) swiped bags and failed attempts. Next is **FRAA** (Fielding Runs Above Average), which also includes the number of games previously played at each position noted in parentheses. Multi-position players have only their two most frequent positions listed here, but their total FRAA number reflects all positions played.

Our last column here is **WARP** (Wins Above Replacement Player). WARP estimates the total value of a player, which means for hitters it takes into account hitting runs above average (calculated using the DRC+ model), BRR and FRAA. Then, it makes an adjustment for positions played and gives the player a credit for plate appearances based upon the difference between "replacement level"¬–which is derived from the quality of players added to a team's roster after the start of the season¬–and the league average.

Catchers

Catchers are a special breed, and thus they have earned their own separate box which displays some of the defensive metrics that we've built just for them. As an example, let's check out J.T. Realmuto.

YEAR	TEAM	P. COUNT	FRM RUNS	BLK RUNS	THRW RUNS	TOT RUNS
2016	MIA	18935	-8.5	1.8	2.1	-5.6
2017	MIA	18959	5.3	1.7	1.0	9.1
2018	MIA	16399	-0.4	0.9	0.1	0.4
2019	PHI	18448	-1.4	1.5	0.7	0.8

The **YEAR** and **TEAM** columns match what you'd find in the other stat box. **P. COUNT** indicates the number of pitches thrown while the catcher was behind the plate, including swinging strikes, fouls, and balls in play. **FRM RUNS** is the total run value the catcher provided (or cost) his team by influencing the umpire to call strikes where other catchers did not. **BLK RUNS** expresses the total run value above or below average for the catcher's ability to prevent wild pitches and passed balls. **THRW RUNS** is calculated using a similar model as the previous two statistics, and it measures a catcher's ability to throw out basestealers but also to dissuade them from testing his arm in the first place. It takes into account factors like the pitcher (including his delivery and pickoff move) and baserunner (who could be as fast as Billy Hamilton or as slow as Yonder Alonso). **TOT RUNS** is the sum of all of the previous three statistics.

Pitchers

Let's give our pitchers a turn, using 2018 NL Cy Young winner Jacob deGrom as our example. Take a look at his first stat block: the first line and the **YEAR**, **TEAM**, **LVL** and **AGE** columns are the same as in the position player example earlier.

Here too, we have a series of columns that display raw, unadjusted statistics compiled by the pitcher over the course of a season: **W** (wins), **L** (losses), **SV** (saves), **G** (games pitched), **GS** (games started), **IP** (innings pitched), **H** (hits allowed) and **HR** (home runs allowed). Next we have two statistics that are rates: **BB/9** (walks per nine innings) and **K/9** (strikeouts per nine innings), before returning to the unadjusted **K** (strikeouts).

Next up is **GB%** (ground ball percentage), which is the percentage of all batted balls that were hit in the ground, including both outs and hits. Remember, this is based on observational data and subject to human error, so please approach this with a healthy dose of skepticism.

BABIP (batting average on balls in play) is calculated using the same methodology as it is for position players, but it often tells us more about a pitcher than it does a hitter. With pitchers, a high BABIP is often due to poor defense or bad luck, and can often be an indicator of potential rebound, and a low BABIP may be cause to expect performance regression. (A typical league-average BABIP is close to .290-.300.)

After a witty 150ish words on the player like only Baseball Prospectus's staff can provide, it's on to that second stat block, which repeats the YEAR, TEAM, LVL, and AGE columns. The metrics **WHIP** (walks plus hits per inning pitched) and **ERA** (earned run average) are old standbys: WHIP measures walks and hits allowed on a per-inning basis, while ERA measures earned runs on a nine-inning basis. Neither of these stats are translated or adjusted.

DRA (Deserved Run Average) was described at length earlier, and measures how many runs the pitcher "deserved" to allow per nine innings. Please note that since we lack all the data points that would make for a "real" DRA for minor-league events, the DRA displayed for minor league partial-seasons is based off of different data. (That data is a modified version of our cFIP metric, which you can find more information about on our website.)

Jacob deGrom   RHP
Born: 06/19/88   Age: 31   Bats: L   Throws: R
Height: 6'4"   Weight: 180   Origin: Round 9, 2010 Draft (#272 overall)

YEAR	TEAM	LVL	AGE	W	L	SV	G	GS	IP	H	HR	BB/9	K/9	K	GB%	BABIP
2016	NYN	MLB	28	7	8	0	24	24	148	142	15	2.2	8.7	143	47%	.312
2017	NYN	MLB	29	15	10	0	31	31	201¹	180	28	2.6	10.7	239	48%	.305
2018	NYN	MLB	30	10	9	0	32	32	217	152	10	1.9	11.2	269	48%	.281
2019	NYN	MLB	31	13	9	0	31	31	186	145	18	2.3	10.7	221	46%	.286

Breakout: 8%   Improve: 29%   Collapse: 28%   Attrition: 6%   MLB: 85%
Comparables: Erik Bedard, A.J. Burnett, CC Sabathia

YEAR	TEAM	LVL	AGE	WHIP	ERA	DRA	WARP	MPH	FB%	WHF	CSP
2016	NYN	MLB	28	1.20	3.04	3.30	3.5	96.3	59.6	12.1	47.2
2017	NYN	MLB	29	1.19	3.53	3.02	5.7	97.2	55.5	14.5	49.5
2018	NYN	MLB	30	0.91	1.70	2.09	8.0	98.2	52.1	16.3	48.4
2019	NYN	MLB	31	1.02	2.91	3.23	3.9	96.6	54.5	14.8	48.2

Just like with hitters, **WARP** (Wins Above Replacement Player) is a total value metric that puts pitchers of all stripes on the same scale as position players. We use DRA as the primary input for our calculation of WARP. You might notice that relief pitchers (due to their limited innings) may have a lower WARP than you were expecting or than you might see in other WARP-like metrics. WARP does not take leverage into account, just the actions a pitcher performs and the expected value of those actions ... which ends up judging high-leverage relief pitchers differently than you might imagine given their prestige and market value.

MPH gives you the pitcher's 95th percentile velocity for the noted season, in order to give you an idea of what the *peak* fastball velocity a pitcher possesses. Since this comes from our pitch tracking data, it is not publicly available for minor-league pitchers.

Finally, we display the three new pitching metrics we described earlier. **FB%** (fastball percentage) gives you the percentage of fastballs thrown out of all pitches. **WhiffRt** (whiff rate) tells you the percentage of swinging strikes induced out of all pitches. **CS Prob** (called strike probability) expresses the likelihood of all pitches thrown to result in a called strike, after controlling for factors like handedness, umpire, pitch type, count, and location.

PECOTA

All players have PECOTA projections for 2019, as well as a set of other numbers that describe the performance of comparable players according to PECOTA. All projections for 2019 are for the player at the date we went to press in early January and are projected into the league and park context as indicated by the team abbreviation. All PECOTA projected statistics represent a player's projected major-league performance.

The numbers beneath the player's stats–Breakout, Improve, Collapse, Attrition–are part and parcel of the PECOTA projections. They estimate the likelihood of changes in performance relative to the player's previously-established level of production, based on the performance of comparable players:

Breakout Rate is the percent change that a player's production will improve by at least 20 percent relative to the weighted average of his performance over his most recent seasons.

Improve Rate is the percent chance that a player's production will improve at all relative to his baseline performance. A player who is expected to perform just the same as he has in the recent past will have an Improve Rate of 50 percent.

Collapse Rate is the percent chance that a position player's production will decline by at least 25 percent relative to his baseline performance.

Attrition Rate operates on playing time rather than performance. Specifically, it measures the likelihood that a player's playing time will decrease by at least 50 percent relative to his established level.

Breakout Rate and Collapse Rate can sometimes be counterintuitive for players who have already experienced a radical change in performance level. It's also worth noting that the projected decline in a player's rate performances might not be indicative of an expected decline in underlying ability or skill, but could just be an anticipated correction following a breakout season.

MLB% is the percentage of similar players who played in the major leagues in their relevant season.

The final pieces of information are the player's three highest-scoring comparable players as determined by PECOTA. All comparables represent a snapshot of how the listed player was performing at the same age as the current player, so if a 23-year-old pitcher is compared to Bartolo Colon, he's actually being compared to a 23-year-old Colon, not the version that pitched for the Rangers in 2018, nor to Colon's career as a whole.

A few points about pitcher projections. First, we aren't yet projecting peak velocity, so that column will be blank in the PECOTA lines. Second, projecting DRA is trickier than evaluating past performance, because it is unclear how deserving each pitcher will be of his anticipated outcomes. However, we know that another DRA-related statistic–contextual FIP or cFIP–estimates future run scoring very well. So for PECOTA, the projected DRA figures you see are based on the past cFIPs generated by the pitcher and comparable players over time, along with the other factors described above.

Lineouts

In each chapter's Lineouts section, you'll find abbreviated text comments, as well as most of same information you'd find in our full player comments. We limit the stats boxes in this section to only including the 2018 information for each player.

Exclusive Player Visualizations

In our constant battle to provide you with new and interesting baseball content you can't find anywhere else, we've added a trio of data visualizations to each hitter's entry in these books and a pair of visualizations for each pitcher.

For hitters, you'll find three new infographics. The first is each player's **Batted Ball Distribution**, which displays the five major sections of the field: LF (left), LCF (left center), CF (center), RCF (right center), and RF (right). The percentage indicated tells us what percentage of batted balls from that hitter fell within that part of the field during the 2018 season. We've also included the hitter's slugging percentage on balls in play (also called **SLGCON**) for that part of the field.

You'll also see two heatmaps: **Strike Zone vs LHP** and **Strike Zone vs RHP**. These heat maps represent a view of the strike zone from behind the catcher. Areas where there is a darker coloration represent the places where a higher percentage of pitches resulted in hits. In other words, the heatmap represents a hitter's "sweet spots" for getting hits against either left-handed or right-handed pitchers, depending on the image.

Pitchers get two images that help explain what their pitches look like from a hitter's perspective: **Pitch Shape vs LHH** and **Pitch Shape vs RHH**. These images show you the shape and the "tunneling" effect of each pitcher's offerings from the batter's perspective. For each type of pitch that a pitcher throws (represented by an indicator shape), there's a set of dots indicating the flight path, where each dot represents a 0.01-second interval. This maps the average trajectory and speed of an offering, ending where the ball crosses the plate. The solid black box represents the regular strike zone, while the gray contour lines indicate the range of locations that a pitcher typically works in.

Below the image, we provide a bit more detailed information about each pitcher's average offering in the **Pitch Types** box. Here, we also list each of the pitcher's major offerings under the **Type** column.

- **Fastballs** (which usually refers to the four-seam variation)
- **Sinkers** and/or two-seam fastballs
- **Cutters** (which could include "hard" cutters like cut fastballs and "soft" cutters that resemble hard sliders)
- **Changeups** (not including most splitters)
- **Splitters** (split-fingered pitches, forkballs, and some split-changes)
- **Sliders** and/or slurves
- **Curveballs** (including spike-curveballs and knuckle-curveballs, as well as some slurvy curves)
- **Slow curveballs** and/or eephus pitches
- **Knuckleballs**
- **Screwballs**

The **Freq** column indicates the percentage of overall pitches that fall into each of those type categories; if a pitcher has a 16.55% score for changeups, then that's the percent of all pitches that he throws as changeups. **Velo** is exactly what you think it is: the average miles per hour for each pitch type. **H Mov** is the number of inches of horizontal movement on the average pitch of that type, while **V Mov** is the number of inches of vertical movement on the average pitch of that type. (At Baseball Prospectus, we measure this over the long flight of the ball and include gravity into the V Mov number in order to give you the most realistic representation of what the pitch *actually* does.)

If you're wondering about the second number in brackets, that's the index for that velocity or movement compared to the league average. Like DRC+, a score of 100 means that the speed or movement is about the same as league average, while a higher score means that there's higher velocity or movement than the league average. Numbers below 100 indicate less velocity or movement than the league average.

Part 1: Team Analysis

Table for Two: Previewing the 2019 Oakland Athletics

Jon Hegglund and Bret Sayre

BRET SAYRE: Hi, Jon. It appears as though we are tasked with making sense of the nonsensical here. Fielding a team more faceless than the House of Black and White, the Athletics will once again do battle with the juggernaut Houston Astros and the perennially disappointing Mike Trouts of Anaheim. There are no other teams left in the AL West, right?

After a magical ride to 97 wins in 2018—the most the franchise had seen since 2002, the year Brad Pitt coaxed them to win 20 games in a row with nothing but his chiseled cheekbones to guide him—PECOTA is basically giving them the "Thank U, Next" treatment. A sub-.500 season would be an awfully disappointing way to follow up a campaign buoyed by multiple breakout players from all walks of the team. So, who's the guy that makes everyone feel silly at year's end for not believing in them?

JON HEGGLUND: Greetings, Bret. I have to say I'm not a fan of the term "breakout," not least because I remember the '80s and it always calls this to mind. So I'm going to begin by counterintuitively asserting that my "breakout" choice will actually perform worse in 2019 than in 2018–and that's Ramon Laureano. The center fielder quickly carved out a reputation as an elite defender based on certain highlight moments, but PECOTA only gives him a 0.6 FRAA, so I'm wondering if our eyes deceive us a little bit.

At the plate, I don't see him getting to the .288/.358/.474 from last year but I think PECOTA is a bit low at .247/.320/.429. He's clearly got the job going into the year, and if he can win the leadoff spot (possibly from "Nick Martini," who is definitely a private detective and not a baseball player), he's looking at a 15/15 season with the on-base skills to elevate him above the Kevin Pillars of the world. "Better than Kevin Pillar": how's that for enthusiasm?

BRET: I mean, it's basically the Beatles on the Ed Sullivan Show over here. But can we go back to Martini for a second? Did he have the best season ever by a player named after a stiff drink?

JON: Well, I've looked into this. Martini posted a 0.9 WARP last year, and the closest I could find was Kris Negron(i)'s 2014, which earned 0.8 WARP. If we expand the adult beverages beyond cocktails, I'm optimistic that Seth Beer will surpass them both within a few years. But back to the team in question: who's your pick for an Athletic that levels up in 2019?

BRET: [says something smart and funny about Franklin Barreto or whatever]

JON: I love PECOTA. I love PECOTA even more with DRC+ baked in. But that doesn't mean there aren't going to be some head scratchers. If it's not revealing too much behind the curtain, there was some internal fretting about the Matt Chapman projection: how does it work that a dude whose batted-ball profile supports *most* of his breakout 2018 second half ends up with a .222/.304/.421—especially given that his almost-thousand major-league plate appearances have yielded a .263/.341/.496 line?

According to PECOTA wizard Jonathan Judge, the key lies in the value that Chapman derives from doubles (he hit 42 last year). Doubles, as one can imagine, are a high-variance outcome: so much depends upon the placement of the batted ball, the skill of the fielders, the speed of the batter, the actions of other baserunners, and so on. So DRC+ regresses doubles heavily, assuming that Chapman's output in 2018 was an outlier. I like that feature of DRC+ in general. And I like that DRC+ does a fantastic job *without* relying on Statcast data. But Statcast measures Chapman as someone who hits the ball hard and is fairly fast–giving some support to the sustainability of his doubles. Long story short: PECOTA may have whiffed on Chapman; we'll see. Was that a rant? Patrick told us not to rant.

So where are you PECOTA-skeptical, Bret?

BRET: Look, it's no secret that I've driving the Jurickson Profar bandwagon the last far-too-many years like Sandra Bullock in Speed, but there was a real offensive breakthrough that finally happened last year. Some of the raw stats may have been slightly inflated by playing in Texas, but April and May were Profar's worst two months of 2018, and his OPS by month after that was .825, .816, .865 and .793. We know PECOTA is paid to be skeptical—he won't shut up about how concerned he is that we're not going to get to see the Clegane Bowl in the final season of Game of Thrones—but I think that the 102 DRC+ and .721 OPS bars are ones he can clear with relative ease for his new team. On the other hand, PECOTA is also strangely high on Profar's defense, so his overall value might not be terribly far off in the end from his projected 2.5 WARP.

The Profar talk also leads us into our natural next question. He was their largest move of the offseason, stepping in to replace Jed Lowrie, and yet the ways in which they've addressed their pitching have been either suspect or sneaky, depending on how much you care about fastball velocity. Which side of 90 are on you on here, Jon? Did the A's do well in addressing their team needs during the offseason or should they have done things differently?

JON: This is a tough question because the current offseason has brought into stark relief the difference between what *we* as writers and fans think teams' aims should be (spend to win! sign free agents!) and what teams' aims actually *are* (maintain "financial flexibility"!). Should the A's have gone after better rotation pieces than Mike Fiers, Marco Estrada, and Brett Anderson? In theory, yes–but is Dallas Keuchel really *that* much better than what they got on the cheap? But maybe all along the plan was to go full Brewers, and bulk up in the pen while trotting out a Potemkin rotation. Despite PECOTA's stank eye, it may work–at least long enough for them to find Jesus… Luzardo, that is.

BRET: If only we all could find a Jesus that pure and holy.

JON: Amen. There's still a corny Dad part of me (well, that's most of me, to be fair) who wants Luzardo to convert to closer for the inevitable "Jesus Saves" joke. That'll be funny for… a minute.

BRET: I mean, I don't know how into Kanye he is, but it's better than the "Jesus Walks" jokes would be.

JON: Bret, I haven't listened to new hip-hop since the third De La Soul album. I've heard of this "Kanye" but your references are lost on me. Back to the A's, though: their team reminds me of something a professor wrote on a paper of mine: "Even when you were wrong, you were *interesting*." That's kind of how I feel about the A's. They may fall to PECOTA's projected mediocrity this year, but they'll always be worth watching.

BRET: You're absolutely right as long as you don't tune in for starting pitchers with good stuff. The bullpen is likely to be one of the best in the American League, and they'll need all of it to overcome the middling arms they'll be announcing over the PA after the National Anthem.

But to answer your other question: Yes, a thousand times yes. In a world where free agency made any sort of sense, Keuchel would be the perfect fit for this team with their strong defensive infield and the fact that the three starters they currently have projected for 20-plus starts are racking up projected wins to the tune of -0.7 WARP. Yes, that negative sign is correct.

JON: Yowch. Well, let's address the elephant in the room, then (get it? Because there's an elephant in their logo?). Do the A's go all Rays-y and use the opener two or three times a week? Or will they still pretend that they have a major-league rotation and sacrifice Daniel Mengden to 25 starts?

BRET: The problem with using the opener only two to three times a week is that they'll have to use one of these starters on those other days. That's… not ideal.

/checks watch again

When is A.J. Puk coming back?

JON: We've got him down for 11 starts, which admittedly might be optimistic, and with a projected 0.7 WARP he still grades out as the second-best starter on the team, behind… Jesus Luzardo. *Ay dios mio!*

OK, you're talking me out of my enthusiasm now, such as it was. This could be a train wreck!

BRET: I guess here's the saving grace then. As much as the starting pitching is wanting when it comes to true talent, they look like they'll be treated as well as reasonably can be expected given how the A's project on defense. And that defense will get quite a workout, as PECOTA doesn't project a single starter of theirs to accumulate more than 122 strikeouts.

If you can't be optimistic coming off a 97-win season, when can you be optimistic?

JON: When Puk and Luzardo are anchoring the rotation, I guess. Until then, the A's will suffer, along with Mindy St. Claire, in the boredom and bad decor of the Medium Place. 81-81, baby. Can't get more medium than that.

Performance Graphs

2018 Hit List Ranking

Committed Payroll (in millions)

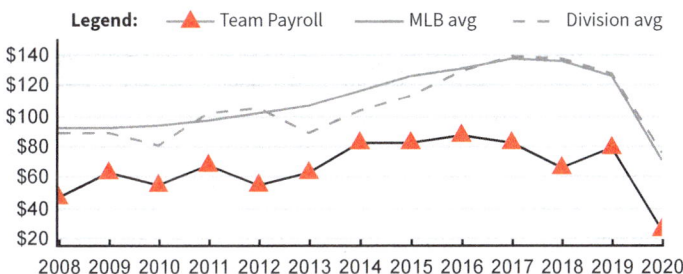

Farm System Ranking

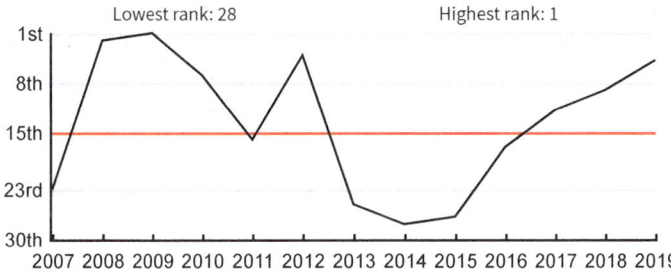

2018 Team Performance

ACTUAL STANDINGS

Team	W	L	Pct
HOU	103	59	.635
OAK	**97**	**65**	**.598**
SEA	89	73	.549
ANA	80	82	.493
TEX	67	95	.413

THIRD-ORDER STANDINGS

Team	W	L	Pct
HOU	108	54	.666
OAK	**96**	**66**	**.592**
SEA	82	80	.506
ANA	80	82	.493
TEX	68	94	.419

TOP HITTERS

Player	WARP
Matt Chapman	6.2
Marcus Semien	5.4
Jed Lowrie	3.9

TOP PITCHERS

Player	WARP
Blake Treinen	2.5
Sean Manaea	2.4
Trevor Cahill	2.3

VITAL STATISTICS

Statistic Name	Value	Rank
Pythagenpat	.588	6th
Runs Scored per Game	5.02	4th
Runs Allowed per Game	4.16	11th
Deserved Runs Created Plus	110	2nd
Deserved Run Average	4.26	12th
Fielding Independent Pitching	4.21	20th
Defensive Efficiency Rating	.730	1st
Batter Age	28.0	15th
Pitcher Age	29.1	21st
Salary	$66.0M	30th
Marginal $ per Marginal Win	$1.1M	30th
Disabled List Days	$1,469.0M	26th
$ on DL	12%	8th

2019 Team Projections

PROJECTED STANDINGS

Team	W	L	Pct	+/-
HOU	98	64	.604	-5
ANA	80	82	.493	0
OAK	**79**	**83**	**.487**	**-18**
TEX	71	91	.438	+4
SEA	70	92	.432	-19

TOP PROJECTED HITTERS

Player	WARP
Matt Chapman	3.3
Khris Davis	3.0
Marcus Semien	2.6

TOP PROJECTED PITCHERS

Player	WARP
Jesus Luzardo	1.1
Blake Treinen	1.1
Liam Hendriks	0.8

FARM SYSTEM REPORT

Top Prospect	Number of Top 101 Prospects
Jesus Luzardo, #13	4

KEY DEDUCTIONS

Player	WARP
Matt Joyce	1.5
Trevor Cahill	1.3
Jed Lowrie	1.3

KEY ADDITIONS

Player	WARP
Jurickson Profar	2.4
Robbie Grossman	1.1
Joakim Soria	0.6

Team Personnel

EVP, Baseball Operations
Billy Beane

General Manager
David Forst

Assistant General Manager
Dan Kantrovitz

Assistant General Manager
Billy Owens

Manager
Bob Melvin

BP Alumni
Al Skorupa

Oakland-Alameda County Coliseum Stats

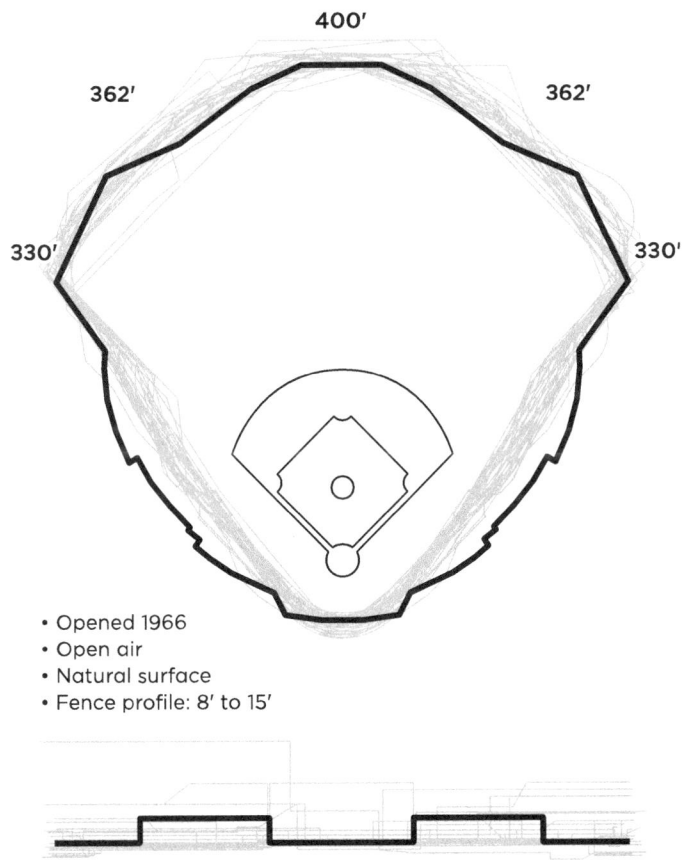

- Opened 1966
- Open air
- Natural surface
- Fence profile: 8' to 15'

Three-Year Park Factors

Runs	Runs/RH	Runs/LH	HR/RH	HR/LH
97	98	96	93	92

Athletics Team Analysis

After three straight last-place finishes, the Oakland A's turned in a surprisingly successful 2018 season, winning 97 games and claiming the second Wild Card spot. But how?

Was the rebuilding team simply a year or two ahead of schedule? Did the "Moneyball" crew figure out some new market inefficiency? Considering the near complete rotation devastation the A's incurred, there was much more at work. It took a number of astute moves to patch things together. Sometimes, that's sheer luck, and Oakland certainly had some of that last season. More often, though, a lot of thought goes into moves: timing promotions and, just as important, demotions, and identifying good fits who might be easily obtained.

That's what the A's front office did so well in 2018, including laying some of the groundwork the previous November when they acquired minor-league outfielder Ramon Laureano from the Astros in exchange for minor-league pitcher Brandon Bailey. "We had asked about him prior to the 2017 season when we had explored some Sonny Gray trades, but he was off limits," A's general manager David Forst said. "We hadn't necessarily followed him closely throughout 2017 but we knew he had a hand injury. … With what we had seen in 2016, it seemed like it was worth a roster spot for us."

The A's had extensive reports on Laureano from special assistant Billy Owens, as well as former Double-A Midland manager Ryan Christenson. Oakland has all minor-league managers turn in evaluations of opposing players, and according to assistant general manager Dan Feinstein, Christenson, now the A's bench coach, stands out when it comes to scouting opponents. Thumbs ups from Owens and Christenson were keys to adding Laureano, and the timing was perfect, with teams needing to protect prospects from the Rule 5 draft and the Astros having a number of top young outfielders—one element of luck for Oakland. Laureano hit .288/.358/.474 in 48 games for the A's.

A similar dynamic came into play with the A's biggest offseason addition. They'd been looking for a right-handed-hitting outfielder under multiple years of team control and the Cardinals, with a glut of outfielders, had a terrific fit: Stephen Piscotty, signed through 2022 with a club option for 2023. There was so much more to this transaction, however. Piscotty is from Pleasanton, not far from Oakland, and his mother, Gretchen, had been diagnosed with ALS, in May. The Cardinals made it clear that if they could trade Piscotty, they'd try to do so to a team near his home. In a rare trade completed at least in part for benevolent reasons, the A's acquired Piscotty on December 14 in exchange for minor-league infielders Yairo Munoz and Max Schrock.

"I think our role in it was increased by the fact that [Cardinals president of baseball operations John Mozeliak] thought it was the right thing to get him closer to home," Forst said. "That being said, the Padres were there with us to the very end, at least that's what we heard. It's not like they were going to move him to us no matter what. ... Our analysis and what we knew of his personal situation led us to believe he could get back to what he did in 2016." Piscotty hit .267/.331/.491 with 27 homers and 41 doubles, topping his 2016 production.

Another outfielder from the St. Louis organization wound up in the A's plans in an under-the-radar deal: They signed Nick Martini as a six-year minor-league free agent based on multiple strong 2017 reports from special assistant Steve Sharpe. "We had him near or at the top of the minor-league free-agent list," Feinstein said. "We reached out to him as soon as we could and were as aggressive as we could be." Martini hit .296/.397/.414 in 55 games for the A's.

For a budget-conscious team, minor-league free agents can be a major plus, so the A's try to cover a lot of bases when looking at the crop each year. "There's one philosophy where we look for guys with upside, and you take some risks on guys who are young. You're looking for major leaguers, you're not just looking for Triple-A depth," Forst said. "We do also target areas of need in the system. With a guy like Martini and Anthony Garcia (another former St. Louis minor leaguer), we thought they could be big leaguers because of what they'd done."

The A's, like everyone else, stockpile as many starting pitchers as possible, but last season tested that almost immediately when Jharel Cotton and A.J. Puk went down with ulnar-collateral ligament tears in March. Oakland turned to two pitchers the front office knew well already, signing former A's Trevor Cahill and Brett Anderson. "There are so many unknowns when you bring players in in free agency or just outside the organization," Forst said. "If you can eliminate some of that uncertainty by dealing with a player who you know, it makes a difference."

Scout Tom Thomas had attended Cahill's February workout, and the A's were in touch with Cahill's agent long before there was a need. It was those two-and-a-half months of conversation that led up to the signing. The conversation with Anderson was more like two-and-a-half minutes. A's vice president of baseball operations Billy Beane simply ran into the left-hander at a Scottsdale gym just as the team was losing pitchers. "Billy assumed Brett had signed somewhere," Forst said. "He asked Brett 'Who are you with?' He said, 'I'm not with anybody.' We know him, so some of that uncertainty is not there. We don't know if he's healthy because he hadn't been."

Once the season began, more starters landed on the disabled list. Daniel Gossett and Kendall Graveman needed Tommy John surgery, Andrew Triggs eventually had thoracic-outlet surgery, Paul Blackburn was out with a forearm issue most of the year, and Cahill and Anderson had a variety of small injuries. Even so, when the A's picked up Edwin Jackson on a minor-league deal after he asked for his release from the Nationals, few noticed. Oakland called up the veteran right-hander on June 25 and the team went 14-3 in his starts. His 3.33 ERA was the sixth-lowest in the league from June 25 on.

Another stroke of good fortune? No. "With Edwin, I wouldn't categorize that as luck because when he was released, Dan [Feinstein] had a relationship with the agent," Forst said. "[Trainer] Nick Paparesta had a relationship with him from Tampa. We knew what we were getting. The timing was really good. We were able to tell him that there might be a big-league opportunity, and we'll let you out if there's not. But … when I saw him throwing 97 at Detroit on TV, I had no idea."

With their depleted rotation, the front office realized the bullpen was the team's strength. Closer Blake Trienen—reacquired as part of the previous summer's Sean Doolittle deal—put up eye-popping numbers. And rookie Lou Trivino worked his way into the setup role, sporting an ERA as low as 1.16 on August 5 before some late-season struggles. "What Lou did, we didn't plan for that," Forst said. "It was such a huge part of our year. We were smart enough to protect him on the 40-man roster, but nobody in this office thought he was going to come up and be our setup guy."

When the trade deadline came around, knowing they didn't want to disrupt their rebuilding efforts by dealing top prospects for a major starter, the A's again looked at the bullpen and dealt for Mets closer Jeurys Familia, Twins closer Fernando Rodney, and Nationals setup man Shawn Kelley. "I think once we got into conversations about trades, we recognized that the acquisition costs and dollars on relievers were going to be more in our range than starters were," Forst said. "The Familia trade happened early. When we made that trade, we weren't yet canvasing everybody. … Rodney was a matter of, he shows up on waivers and we're still looking for help. He's really good, let's throw in a waiver claim and see what happens."

The Kelley move was unusual, as the A's took advantage of the fact that the Nationals had dumped him after an on-field snit-fit during a blowout. And then Oakland took a calculated risk, waiting him out on waivers. "With Kelley, we had talked to [Nationals general manager] Mike Rizzo about him before that incident," Forst said. "It was opportunistic when we saw what happened there and they designated him. We talked about him on trade waivers but we didn't put in the claim, hoping he would get through and we could get him for the minimum salary."

The A's also added starter Mike Fiers in a waiver deal with Detroit, with the team winning eight of his nine starts. They had held some talks with the Tigers before the deadline, but couldn't consummate a deal. The A's lucked out when Fiers fell to them on the waiver wire, surprising many around baseball who'd assumed the Mariners would claim him. "The fact that Fiers got to us on trade waivers, that was lucky," Forst said. "We had the foundation and the conversation in place because we talked about him before the deadline and we had also already talked to ownership about adding the money. All that stuff was in place when we did get the claim."

The biggest addition Oakland made that month, however, may have been Laureano, called up on August 3. Center field was the one unsettled spot in the A's lineup. They had fully intended for Dustin Fowler, acquired from the Yankees in the Sonny Gray deal, to fill the job long term, but he'd missed almost the entire year after a horrific knee injury and, after a promising start when first called up, he'd tailed off. Fowler's inexperience and the previous year's layoff was showing.

"That combination on Dustin was tough," Forst said. "Any time you have a young player, you want to bring them to the big leagues when they're over-ready and when they're performing really well so they can get off on the right foot. ... It's not a science. You're just trying to figure out the right time. ... We've talked about that going all the way back to Ben Grieve and Miguel Tejada and Eric Chavez. When you get someone here, you want them to stay. It doesn't always work out that way. It didn't with Matt Olson, for instance. Dustin was new to the organization effectively and you want to make sure you're respectful of his ego and feelings and all these things that go into those decisions when he's going up and down."

Laureano was batting .297 at Nashville, and his defensive work was off the charts. Every report the front office got was glowing. Nashville manager Fran Riordan was texting proof regularly. "Ramon was playing so well that we just couldn't keep him there any longer," Forst said. "Fran was sending us video on his assists from the outfield. From the minute he got there out of extended spring, they were raving about everything: How hard he plays, how great he is in the outfield. It was immediately noticed the impact he could make."

Laureano hit .288 the rest of the way, with five homers and seven steals in 32 starts. Most importantly: He turned in the best center-field defense the A's have seen in a long time and made one of the plays of the year on August 11, racing into the left-center gap for a Justin Upton drive and then turning and firing to first base—on the fly—to double off Eric Young Jr. Martini, too, turned out to be a nice fit as the team's left-handed-hitting leadoff man. He was playing so well, in fact, that it was surprising when he was optioned out on August 30 with the A's still trying to nail down a playoff spot.

As it turns out, this was one transaction the A's flubbed. They believed they could assign Martini to a minor-league team that was wrapping up its season and he would return before the 10-day limit was up. That rule, however, had changed in the most recent CBA—players optioned out before rosters expand in September can't return for 10 days, no matter where they're assigned. Forst took immediate responsibility for the gaffe—and, worse, he said in a November interview, A's travel secretary Mickey Morabito had warned the front office about the CBA change. "We screwed up," Forst said. "Mickey told me the rule five days before that, and I blew him off. I said, 'You're wrong,' without looking it up."

Ultimately, much of the A's success came down to that carefully constructed bullpen. They were undefeated when leading after seven innings into the final week of the season and finished 70-2 in such games. The bullpen's ERA was 3.00 from June 3 on. Oakland relievers earned 45 wins, the second-most in major-league history behind the 2018 Rays with 55—and when Manaea landed on the DL in August, the A's took a page from Tampa Bay's handbook and began using an "opener," reliever Liam Hendriks, when he was called up September 1. Hendriks was another oddity of a transaction. He'd been designated for assignment on June 25 with an ERA over 7.00, but he cleared waivers and got his act back together at Triple-A.

Once out of the picture, Hendriks was pitching the first inning for the A's once or twice a week in the middle of the pennant race. "Things were going so well at the back end of the bullpen with Rodney, Familia and Trivino. Everybody had a role," Forst said, adding that manager Bob Melvin didn't want to disrupt that dynamic. "The next-best place to get the most out of Liam was in the first inning. He was pitching really well. How do we fit him in because we don't want to use him just to mop up? We were down a starter, so let's get him in some high-leverage spots in the first inning."

Hendriks thrived, with a 1.38 ERA and a .178 opponents average. And somehow, someway, it was Hendriks, the once-abandoned Australian, opening in the Wild Card game at Yankee Stadium. New York got two quick runs off Hendriks when Aaron Judge smacked a two-run homer, but it was other relievers working much earlier than usual who really struggled; Rodney and Treinen combined to allow five runs.

"Right up until it didn't work, it was great," Forst said of the A's bullpenning experiment, adding that the team might continue to tinker with the strategy, depending on the personnel. "I think from the standpoint of the first inning, where scoring is the highest and you're facing the best hitters, it was really successful. Maybe the next part of the equation is making sure the mindset is right coming in after."

After the season, Beane was named the Major League Executive of the Year, reflecting the remarkable work by the entire front office. Forst received a four-year contract extension, through 2023, recognition that the story of the A's terrific season was one of many small transactions here and there, many under the radar. When lots of small decisions pay off, that can make all the difference for a team with limited resources, and in 2018 those moves fueled one of the more remarkable turnarounds in A's history.

—*Susan Slusser is a writer at the San Francisco Chronicle.*

Part 2: Player Analysis

Franklin Barreto MI

Born: 02/27/96 Age: 23 Bats: R Throws: R
Height: 5'10" Weight: 190 Origin: International Free Agent, 2012

YEAR	TEAM	LVL	AGE	PA	R	2B	3B	HR	RBI	BB	K	SB	CS	AVG/OBP/SLG
2016	MID	AA	20	507	63	25	3	10	50	36	90	30	15	.281/.340/.413
2017	NAS	AAA	21	510	63	19	7	15	54	27	141	15	8	.290/.339/.456
2017	OAK	MLB	21	76	10	1	2	2	6	5	33	2	0	.197/.250/.352
2018	NAS	AAA	22	333	54	16	1	18	46	39	106	5	2	.259/.357/.514
2018	OAK	MLB	22	75	10	4	0	5	16	1	29	0	0	.233/.253/.493
2019	OAK	MLB	23	204	25	8	1	7	23	11	60	4	2	.239/.291/.404

Breakout: 17% Improve: 37% Collapse: 6% Attrition: 20% MLB: 63%
Comparables: Arismendy Alcantara, Dilson Herrera, Yoan Moncada

The five homers in 75 plate appearances Barreto put up in sporadic major-league time last year is around a 40-dinger pace for a full season, which is why everyone's still excited for him to arrive even though it seems like the wait has been forever. He's still just 23, though, and it's not his fault Jed Lowrie somehow figured out, in his mid-30s, how to stay healthy. Barreto was always a bat-to-ball prospect, but he seems to have traded that off (32 percent strikeout rate the last two years vs. 19 percent in 2013–16) in order to knock more balls out of the yard (a homer every 24 plate appearances vs. every 43). He is also a card-carrying member of the Fly Ball Revolution: The average launch angle of his balls in play last year was akin to Brian McCann's, who has a well-known affection for worms. That said, if Barreto is going to earn and keep a full-time job, he will need to start spitting on more pitches outside the zone, lest he find himself in Salvador Perez territory, simply not receiving enough hittable offerings to do damage.

YEAR	TEAM	LVL	AGE	PA	DRC+	VORP	BABIP	BRR	FRAA	WARP
2016	MID	AA	20	507	113	27.5	.330	3.1	SS(81): -10.7, 2B(33): -3.1	0.4
2017	NAS	AAA	21	510	105	34.6	.384	0.3	SS(83): -3.3, 2B(25): -2.6	1.3
2017	OAK	MLB	21	76	55	0.2	.333	0.7	SS(11): 0.3, 2B(10): 0.2	0.0
2018	NAS	AAA	22	333	128	35.6	.337	3.5	2B(60): -2.2, SS(11): 0.4	1.9
2018	OAK	MLB	22	75	76	-0.8	.308	-1.1	2B(26): -1.7, SS(2): 0.0	-0.3
2019	OAK	MLB	23	204	88	4.7	.309	0.1	2B -3, SS 0	0.1

Franklin Barreto, continued

Batted Ball Distribution

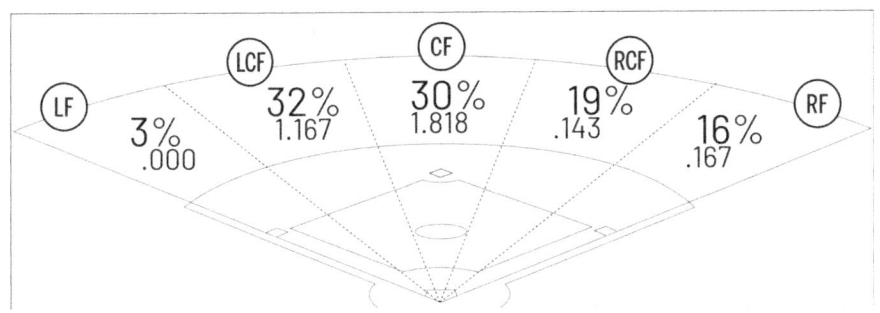

Strike Zone vs LHP   Strike Zone vs RHP

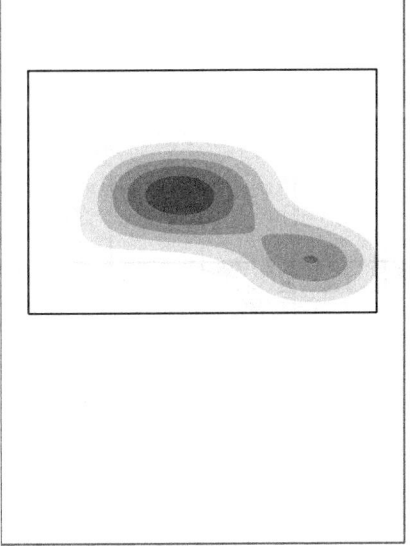

Mark Canha OF

Born: 02/15/89 Age: 30 Bats: R Throws: R
Height: 6'2" Weight: 210 Origin: Round 7, 2010 Draft (#227 overall)

YEAR	TEAM	LVL	AGE	PA	R	2B	3B	HR	RBI	BB	K	SB	CS	AVG/OBP/SLG
2016	OAK	MLB	27	44	4	0	0	3	6	0	20	0	1	.122/.140/.341
2017	NAS	AAA	28	317	52	25	3	12	50	34	62	4	0	.283/.373/.529
2017	OAK	MLB	28	187	16	13	1	5	14	7	56	2	0	.208/.262/.382
2018	OAK	MLB	29	411	60	22	0	17	52	34	88	1	2	.249/.328/.449
2019	OAK	MLB	30	192	22	10	1	6	22	15	45	1	1	.238/.312/.413

Breakout: 7% Improve: 43% Collapse: 22% Attrition: 11% MLB: 99%
Comparables: Lorenzo Cain, Charlie Blackmon, Brennan Boesch

In last year's book, we posited that Canha did not have the requisite power to be a major-league player given that he was limited to the three easiest defensive positions. The obvious conclusion to draw from Canha's emergence last year is that he took motivation from us. You're welcome, A's fans. Canha's overall batting line ended just about even with the average major-league right fielder even as he took on a team-leading 466 innings of work in center field, where he performed somewhere in that nebulous "not unwatchable, but not exactly *capable* either" realm that signifies an unspoken "well, what the hell else do you want me to do?" from the manager while gesturing at the roster. Canha's hitting was driven by a .604 slugging percentage against lefties that was frightfully close to his .665 *OPS* against right-handers. That will probably keep him rosterable, or at least on the shuttle squad, for one more year, helped along by the A's burning only two of his option years so far.

YEAR	TEAM	LVL	AGE	PA	DRC+	VORP	BABIP	BRR	FRAA	WARP
2016	OAK	MLB	27	44	65	-3.6	.105	-0.1	1B(5): 0.2, LF(3): -0.1	-0.1
2017	NAS	AAA	28	317	140	33.0	.323	3.3	RF(61): -2.7, CF(8): 0.9	1.9
2017	OAK	MLB	28	187	67	-2.9	.274	0.3	RF(22): -1.0, LF(20): -0.9	-0.6
2018	OAK	MLB	29	411	115	19.2	.282	-0.3	CF(62): -5.9, LF(51): 1.4	1.5
2019	OAK	MLB	30	192	106	6.2	.285	-0.3	LF 1, 1B -1	0.6

Mark Canha, continued

Batted Ball Distribution

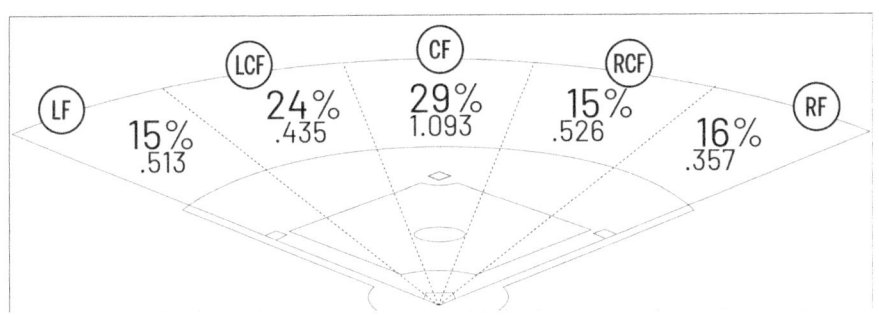

Strike Zone vs LHP **Strike Zone vs RHP**

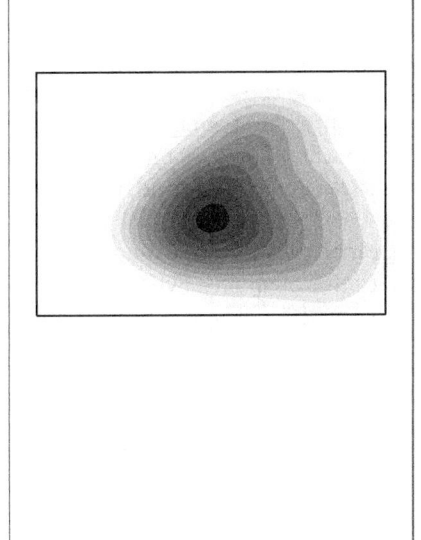

Matt Chapman 3B

Born: 04/28/93 Age: 26 Bats: R Throws: R
Height: 6'0" Weight: 210 Origin: Round 1, 2014 Draft (#25 overall)

YEAR	TEAM	LVL	AGE	PA	R	2B	3B	HR	RBI	BB	K	SB	CS	AVG/OBP/SLG
2016	MID	AA	23	504	78	26	4	29	83	59	147	7	4	.244/.335/.521
2016	NAS	AAA	23	85	14	1	1	7	13	9	26	0	0	.197/.282/.513
2017	NAS	AAA	24	204	30	6	2	16	30	25	63	5	4	.257/.348/.589
2017	OAK	MLB	24	326	39	23	2	14	40	32	92	0	3	.234/.313/.472
2018	OAK	MLB	25	616	100	42	6	24	68	58	146	1	2	.278/.356/.508
2019	OAK	MLB	26	610	79	26	3	25	72	59	162	3	3	.220/.302/.418

Breakout: 5% Improve: 50% Collapse: 13% Attrition: 13% MLB: 96%
Comparables: Chris Davis, Ian Stewart, Pedro Alvarez

How was Chapman going to follow up a star-level half-season rookie performance that featured light-tower power, flashy defense and way too many whiffs? Why, by keeping the power and defense while chopping five percentage points off the strikeout rate, because everything always goes well and nothing is bad. Taking that step forward and doing it over a full season of playing time pushed Chapman to 11th in baseball in BWARP. Unfortunately for his notoriety, but fortunately for fans of great baseball, nine of the 10 ahead of him were 27 or younger and three of them were fellow third basemen (Jose Ramirez, Alex Bregman, Nolan Arenado, plus whatever Manny Machado is now). Chapman's season wound up strikingly similar to the 2014 line of the last Oakland superstar, Josh Donaldson; that name is bound to raise bitter feelings in A's fans because Donaldson was traded that winter. The difference, though, is that Chapman is two years younger than Donaldson was, and two years away from arbitration eligibility. Even if the A's cannot figure out their ballpark situation, or if they do get a new park but continue their bargain-basement ways anyway, there should still be another couple of years for the Oakland faithful to enjoy Chapman's cannon arm and balls-out, headlong sprints for foul popups.

YEAR	TEAM	LVL	AGE	PA	DRC+	VORP	BABIP	BRR	FRAA	WARP
2016	MID	AA	23	504	128	35.4	.293	1.8	3B(100): 14.6, SS(10): 3.6	4.3
2016	NAS	AAA	23	85	108	6.7	.186	0.2	3B(18): 2.1	0.5
2017	NAS	AAA	24	204	133	20.6	.293	-0.1	3B(49): 7.2	1.9
2017	OAK	MLB	24	326	97	14.1	.290	-1.0	3B(84): 12.6	2.2
2018	OAK	MLB	25	616	125	48.4	.338	3.8	3B(145): 15.6	6.2
2019	OAK	MLB	26	610	100	17.0	.266	-1.1	3B 19	3.3

Matt Chapman, continued

Batted Ball Distribution

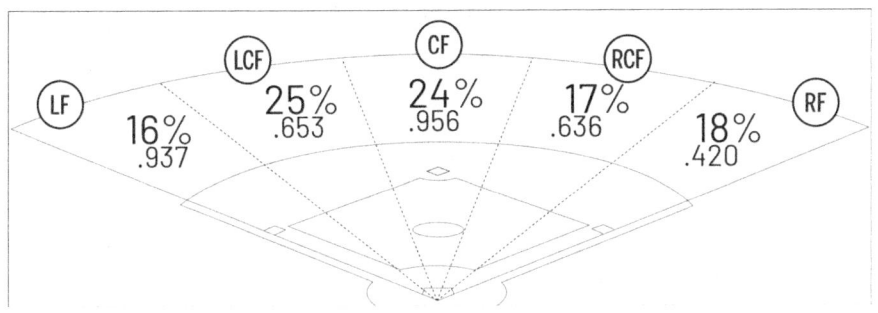

Strike Zone vs LHP

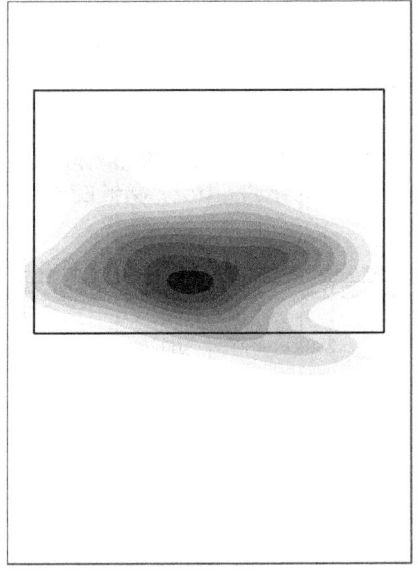

Strike Zone vs RHP

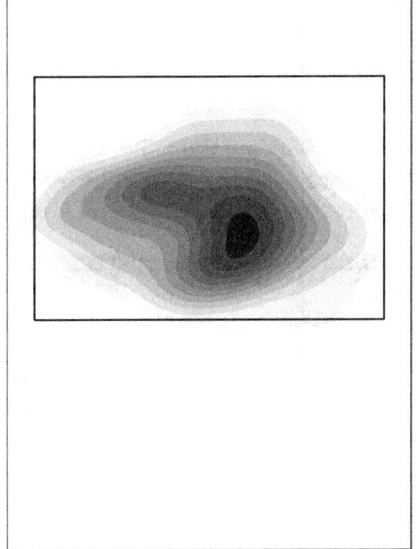

Khris Davis DH

Born: 12/21/87   Age: 31   Bats: R   Throws: R
Height: 5'10"   Weight: 195   Origin: Round 7, 2009 Draft (#226 overall)

YEAR	TEAM	LVL	AGE	PA	R	2B	3B	HR	RBI	BB	K	SB	CS	AVG/OBP/SLG
2016	OAK	MLB	28	610	85	24	2	42	102	42	166	1	2	.247/.307/.524
2017	OAK	MLB	29	652	91	28	1	43	110	73	195	4	0	.247/.336/.528
2018	OAK	MLB	30	654	98	28	1	48	123	59	175	0	0	.247/.326/.549
2019	OAK	MLB	31	626	84	28	1	34	96	62	168	2	1	.245/.327/.484

Breakout: 2%   Improve: 25%   Collapse: 25%   Attrition: 8%   MLB: 96%
Comparables: Eric Thames, Fred McGriff, Richie Sexson

The A's finally made Davis a full-time designated hitter last year, and reaped the reward, adding nearly a full win to Davis' WARP while running out a generally solid goulash of left fielders (Pinder, Joyce, Martini, Canha) in his place. Davis continued to do what he always does at the plate: hit .247 (his fourth straight year at that figure, indisputable proof of a benevolent higher power with a sharp sense of humor) and smack 40-plus dingers (his third straight season, and a new career high). He's the rare bat-only player worth a multi-year commitment, even though he costs you the ability to use the DH as a half-rest spot for other players, and even if we should look at Chris Davis' age-30 to -32 seasons for a sense of the downside.

Davis' Wild Card Game homer against the Yankees left him in a four-way tie for the best career homers-per-playoff-game rate in baseball history, with Eddie Rosario, Mark Trumbo and Mark Brouhard.

YEAR	TEAM	LVL	AGE	PA	DRC+	VORP	BABIP	BRR	FRAA	WARP
2016	OAK	MLB	28	610	125	23.9	.270	-3.3	LF(93): 0.2	2.8
2017	OAK	MLB	29	652	123	32.5	.290	-0.2	LF(116): -8.9	2.5
2018	OAK	MLB	30	654	139	34.0	.261	-4.6	LF(11): -1.9	3.4
2019	OAK	MLB	31	626	124	26.8	.287	-1.0		3.0

Khris Davis, continued

Batted Ball Distribution

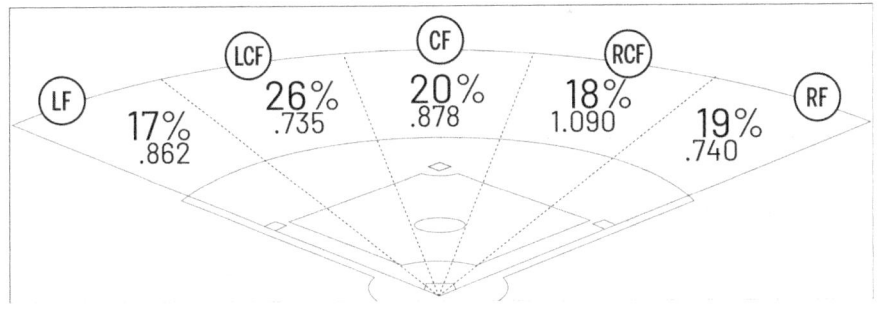

Strike Zone vs LHP

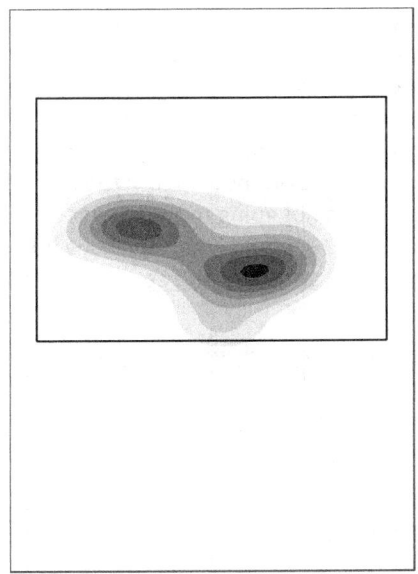

Strike Zone vs RHP

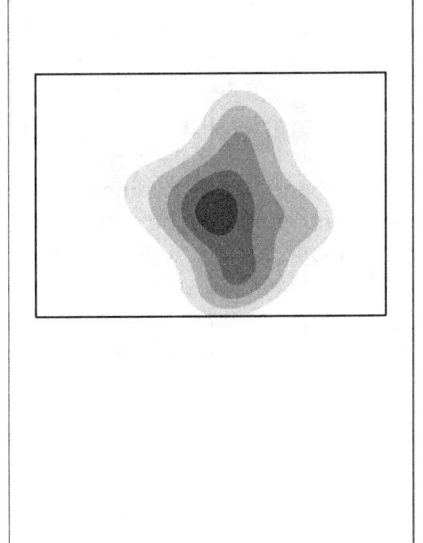

Dustin Fowler CF

Born: 12/29/94 Age: 24 Bats: L Throws: L
Height: 6'0" Weight: 195 Origin: Round 18, 2013 Draft (#554 overall)

YEAR	TEAM	LVL	AGE	PA	R	2B	3B	HR	RBI	BB	K	SB	CS	AVG/OBP/SLG
2016	TRN	AA	21	574	67	30	15	12	88	22	86	25	11	.281/.311/.458
2017	SWB	AAA	22	313	49	19	8	13	43	15	63	13	5	.293/.329/.542
2018	NAS	AAA	23	239	37	17	6	4	27	9	41	13	2	.341/.364/.520
2018	OAK	MLB	23	203	19	3	2	6	23	8	47	6	4	.224/.256/.354
2019	OAK	MLB	24	222	27	11	2	6	23	10	48	8	3	.249/.288/.407

Breakout: 21% Improve: 55% Collapse: 6% Attrition: 27% MLB: 74%
Comparables: Josh Reddick, Nate Schierholtz, Raimel Tapia

Fowler returned from the brutal knee injury that ended his 2017 season, but lost a spring battle for the A's center-field job to a Boog Powell-Jake Smolinski platoon. When Powell got hurt early on, and with Smolinski not hitting, Oakland turned largely to erstwhile first baseman Mark Canha to man the position. None of this speaks well of Fowler's standing with the A's brass. He came to the majors and joined a platoon with Canha in mid-May, but proceeded to justify the April decisions by putting up the batting line you see above. While Fowler had a reputation for aggression, and his walk rate appears to back that, the issue was less chasing bad pitches and more that pitchers weren't afraid of him: Among players with at least 100 plate appearances, he was in the top five percent of pitches seen in the strike zone. If Fowler can't figure out how to turn those strikes around for at *least* line-drive doubles, he's not going to be a major leaguer, not given that he's merely passable in center field, and especially now that Ramon Laureano took advantage of Fowler's struggles and seized the job in August and September.

YEAR	TEAM	LVL	AGE	PA	DRC+	VORP	BABIP	BRR	FRAA	WARP
2016	TRN	AA	21	574	103	29.1	.313	3.5	CF(119): -9.7, RF(3): -0.6	0.2
2017	SWB	AAA	22	313	121	18.5	.335	-0.7	CF(40): -4.5, RF(14): -1.1	0.6
2018	NAS	AAA	23	239	122	24.4	.400	0.2	CF(51): -12.9, LF(2): 0.6	-0.1
2018	OAK	MLB	23	203	84	-3.2	.262	-1.0	CF(57): -3.8, RF(3): -0.1	-0.2
2019	OAK	MLB	24	222	90	5.5	.296	0.8	CF -5, LF 0	0.2

Dustin Fowler, continued

Batted Ball Distribution

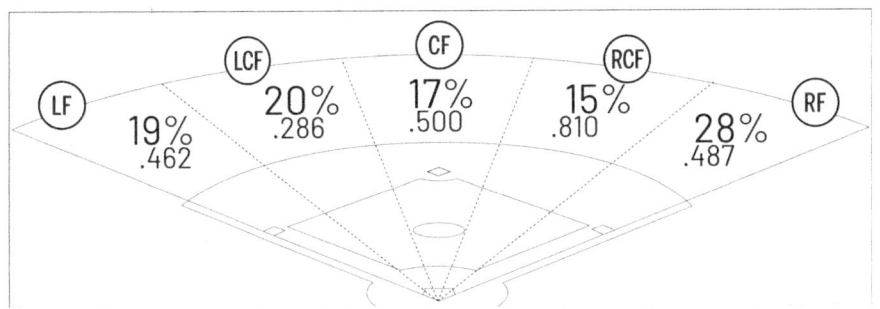

Strike Zone vs LHP   **Strike Zone vs RHP**

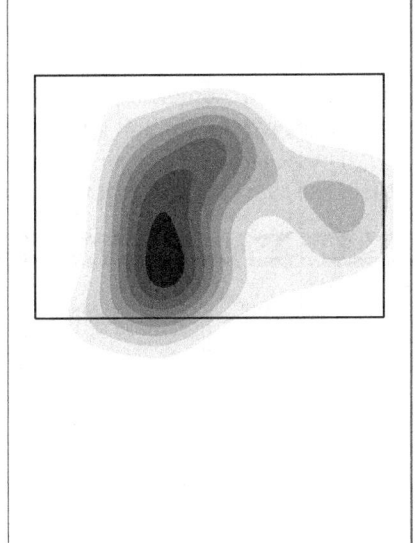

Robbie Grossman RF

Born: 09/16/89 Age: 29 Bats: B Throws: L
Height: 6'0" Weight: 215 Origin: Round 6, 2008 Draft (#174 overall)

YEAR	TEAM	LVL	AGE	PA	R	2B	3B	HR	RBI	BB	K	SB	CS	AVG/OBP/SLG
2016	COH	AAA	26	139	14	5	0	6	13	21	25	3	1	.256/.370/.453
2016	MIN	MLB	26	389	49	19	1	11	37	55	96	2	3	.280/.386/.443
2017	MIN	MLB	27	456	62	22	1	9	45	67	79	3	1	.246/.361/.380
2018	MIN	MLB	28	465	50	27	1	5	48	60	83	0	1	.273/.367/.384
2019	OAK	MLB	29	391	41	19	1	7	39	47	77	2	1	.246/.341/.370

Breakout: 3% Improve: 41% Collapse: 14% Attrition: 19% MLB: 93%
Comparables: Chris Coghlan, Gabe Gross, Chris Burke

In one of the stories of *Winnie-the-Pooh*, Rabbit asks Pooh if he made up a particular song that Pooh had been singing. Pooh says he only sort of did — that sometimes, things just come to him. Rabbit waves away that answer, on his way to some other subject, because (as the narrator points out) Rabbit "never let things come to him, but rather went and fetched them." In today's game, Grossman is a Pooh, in a league full of Rabbits. He's excruciatingly patient, and when the right sequence of unworthy pitches comes along, he's quite good at going with them and creating something good, be it a walk, a double into the corner or a cheap homer. Most of the time, however, the competitive landscape of the league rewards Rabbit types, because today's pitchers don't make enough mistakes to let a Pooh like Grossman really thrive. He also plays the outfield like there's a honey pot over his head.

YEAR	TEAM	LVL	AGE	PA	DRC+	VORP	BABIP	BRR	FRAA	WARP
2016	COH	AAA	26	139	119	5.4	.279	-1.6	CF(19): -1.4, LF(10): 1.8	0.4
2016	MIN	MLB	26	389	118	18.0	.364	-0.2	LF(75): -5.4, CF(1): 0.0	1.1
2017	MIN	MLB	27	456	99	5.0	.287	-1.9	RF(35): -1.6, LF(18): -1.2	0.3
2018	MIN	MLB	28	465	105	13.1	.329	-4.9	RF(52): -2.6, LF(34): 1.2	0.6
2019	OAK	MLB	29	391	102	11.7	.295	-0.8	LF -1	1.1

Robbie Grossman, continued

Batted Ball Distribution

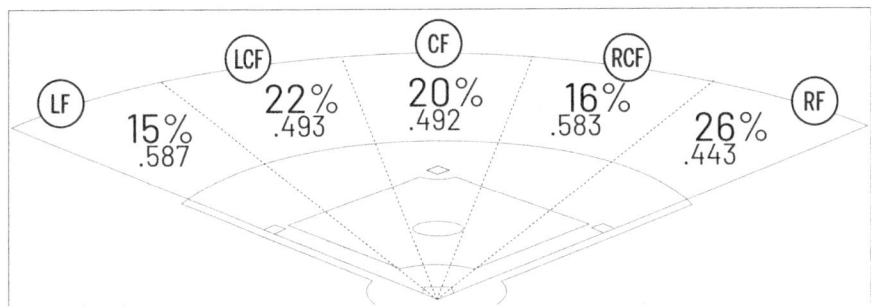

Strike Zone vs LHP

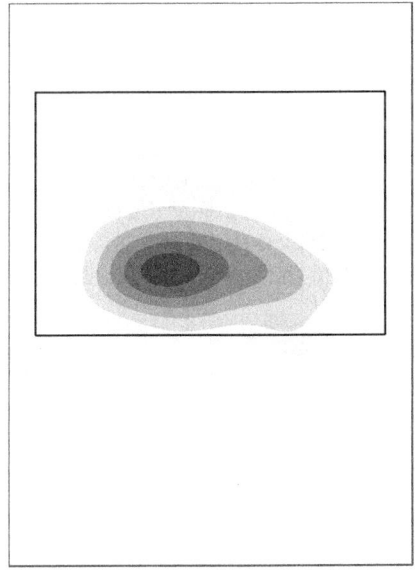

Strike Zone vs RHP

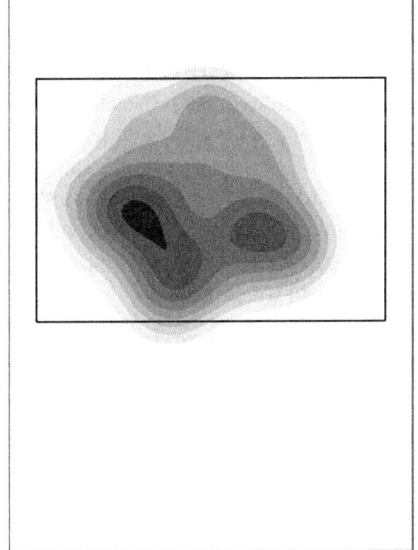

Nick Hundley C
Born: 09/08/83   Age: 35   Bats: R   Throws: R
Height: 6'0"   Weight: 203   Origin: Round 2, 2005 Draft (#76 overall)

YEAR	TEAM	LVL	AGE	PA	R	2B	3B	HR	RBI	BB	K	SB	CS	AVG/OBP/SLG
2016	COL	MLB	32	317	30	20	1	10	48	25	65	0	0	.260/.320/.439
2017	SFN	MLB	33	303	27	23	0	9	35	12	81	0	0	.244/.272/.418
2018	SFN	MLB	34	305	34	13	2	10	31	22	85	2	1	.241/.298/.408
2019	OAK	MLB	35	213	21	11	1	5	23	15	54	1	1	.241/.297/.385

Breakout: 3%   Improve: 16%   Collapse: 39%   Attrition: 20%   MLB: 88%
Comparables: Benito Santiago, Terry Steinbach, Ivan Rodriguez

Hundley is a master of the intangible. He calls a good game. He gives you a quality at-bat. He steers his batterymates through trouble, be it a bases-loaded jam or a benches-clearing brawl. Revered in the press box and the broadcast booth, he's a pro's pro, a future manager, the preferred backup catcher of a bygone era when his shortcomings were as immeasurable as his strengths. As catching moves from art to science, each new metric stains Hundley's reputation. He's below average in every quantifiable facet of catcher defense: a poor blocker, a weak thrower, one of the very worst framers in the league. We'd feel worse if Hundley were 25 and not 35, for at least his skills are being devalued near the sunset of his playing career. It won't be long before today's Nick Hundleys are managing tomorrow's Sandy Leons. He'll be well prepared for that next chapter when he's ready to turn the page.

YEAR	TEAM	P. COUNT	FRM RUNS	BLK RUNS	THRW RUNS	TOT RUNS
2016	COL	11523	-9.3	0.0	-3.2	-13.2
2017	SFN	10101	-1.1	0.0	0.6	-1.1
2018	SFN	10802	-13.2	-0.5	-0.3	-14.1
2019	OAK	7934	-7.2	-0.1	-0.6	-7.9

YEAR	TEAM	LVL	AGE	PA	DRC+	VORP	BABIP	BRR	FRAA	WARP
2016	COL	MLB	32	317	90	12.8	.302	-0.3	C(79): -12.8	-0.2
2017	SFN	MLB	33	303	76	8.8	.307	-2.8	C(82): -0.9	0.2
2018	SFN	MLB	34	305	89	10.3	.310	0.1	C(83): -14.0	-0.4
2019	OAK	MLB	35	213	81	4.5	.298	-0.4	C -9	-0.6

Nick Hundley, continued

Batted Ball Distribution

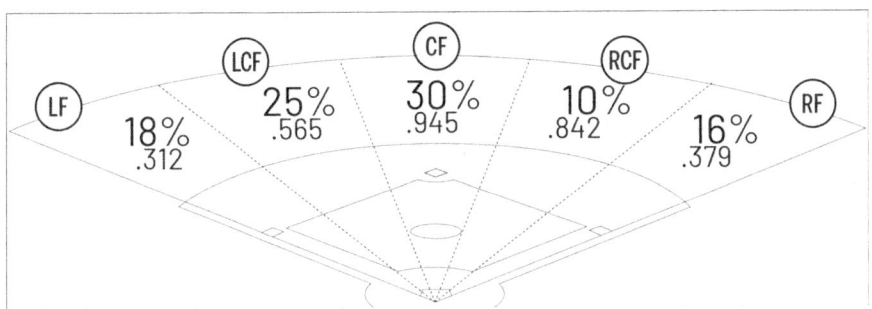

Strike Zone vs LHP

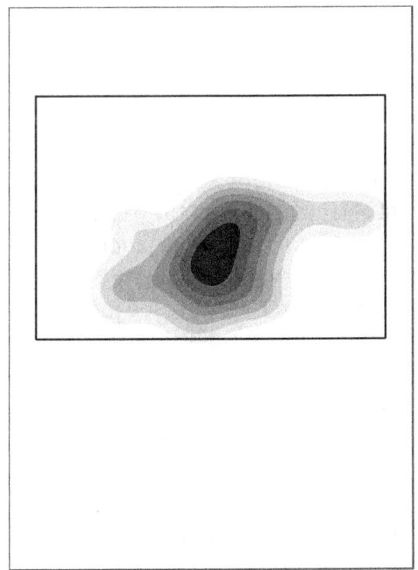

Strike Zone vs RHP

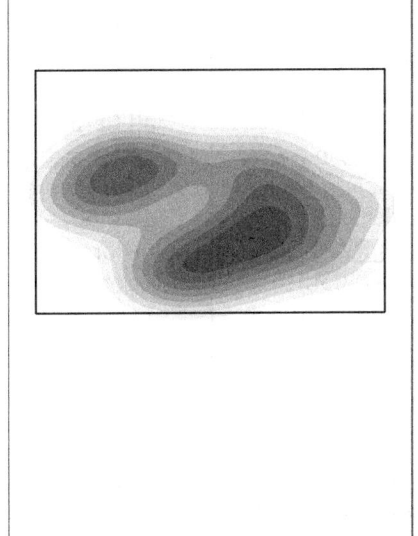

Ramon Laureano CF

Born: 07/15/94   Age: 24   Bats: R   Throws: R
Height: 5'11"   Weight: 185   Origin: Round 16, 2014 Draft (#466 overall)

YEAR	TEAM	LVL	AGE	PA	R	2B	3B	HR	RBI	BB	K	SB	CS	AVG/OBP/SLG
2016	LNC	A+	21	357	69	19	5	10	60	50	86	33	11	.317/.426/.519
2016	CCH	AA	21	148	20	9	2	5	13	20	33	10	3	.323/.432/.548
2017	CCH	AA	22	513	65	21	6	11	55	40	110	24	5	.227/.298/.369
2018	NAS	AAA	23	284	44	12	1	14	35	31	70	11	2	.297/.380/.524
2018	OAK	MLB	23	176	27	12	1	5	19	16	50	7	1	.288/.358/.474
2019	OAK	MLB	24	490	66	21	2	18	58	43	132	18	4	.247/.319/.427

Breakout: 11%   Improve: 40%   Collapse: 17%   Attrition: 21%   MLB: 76%
Comparables: Derek Fisher, Joe Benson, Lewis Brinson

If Laureano is really a star, which is how he played over the last two months of 2018, here's who missed on him: the amateur scouts, who didn't draft him out of high school and popped him in the 16th round after two years in junior college; the Astros' talent evaluators, who added relief pitchers Cionel Perez and Dean Deetz to the 40-man roster rather than Laureano; 28 other teams, which weren't willing to give up more than the low-level pitching prospect the A's sent to Houston in trade; and every major public talent evaluator, including here at BP, none of whom put Laureano on a top-100 list. Stars do get missed! Jose Ramirez, J.D. Martinez, Matt Carpenter, Justin Turner and DJ LeMahieu all finished in the top 20 in BWARP last year without ever appearing on a top-100 prospect list. Turner, Martinez, Ramirez and LeMahieu scuffled for years in the majors before breaking out, though; it's the *immediate* impact by a non-elite prospect that makes the performance so hard to believe. (Though there's always Carpenter.) The point here is not that Laureano isn't a big leaguer: The defense is real, and he's always shown good command of the strike zone and enough power to make pitchers work. Just think more his September line (.269/.343/.441) than August (.317/.380/.524). That's more or less what George Springer hit in 2018, after all, and it meant he was a solidly above-average player.

YEAR	TEAM	LVL	AGE	PA	DRC+	VORP	BABIP	BRR	FRAA	WARP
2016	LNC	A+	21	357	158	35.2	.411	1.2	CF(30): 4.5, RF(23): 3.8	3.3
2016	CCH	AA	21	148	168	18.9	.407	1.0	CF(20): 3.6, RF(15): 3.1	2.0
2017	CCH	AA	22	513	82	11.6	.273	6.3	RF(95): 7.8, CF(31): -1.7	0.3
2018	NAS	AAA	23	284	144	24.2	.358	1.7	RF(45): 6.2, CF(19): -0.5	2.5
2018	OAK	MLB	23	176	93	16.2	.388	1.4	CF(47): 3.0	0.9
2019	OAK	MLB	24	490	103	23.6	.307	1.9	CF 1	2.4

Ramon Laureano, continued

Batted Ball Distribution

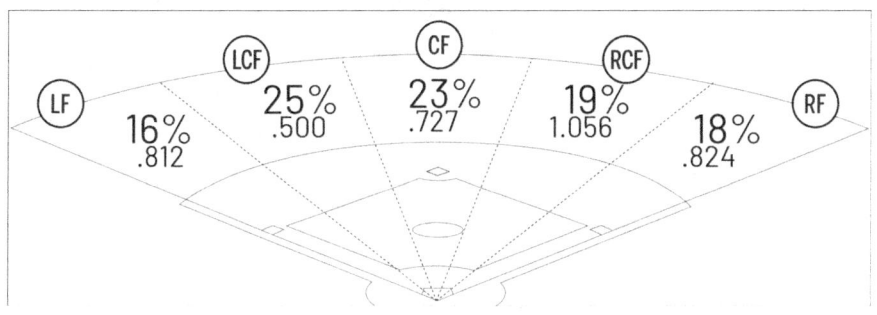

Strike Zone vs LHP

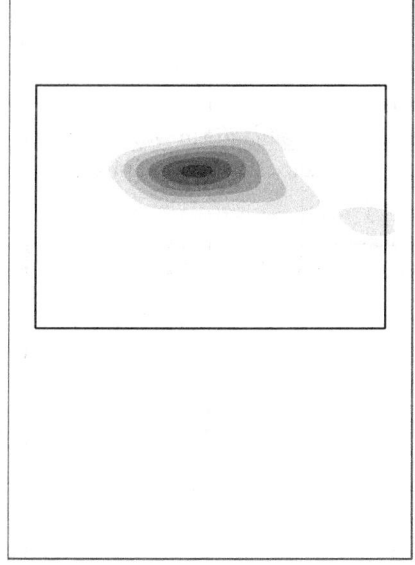

Strike Zone vs RHP

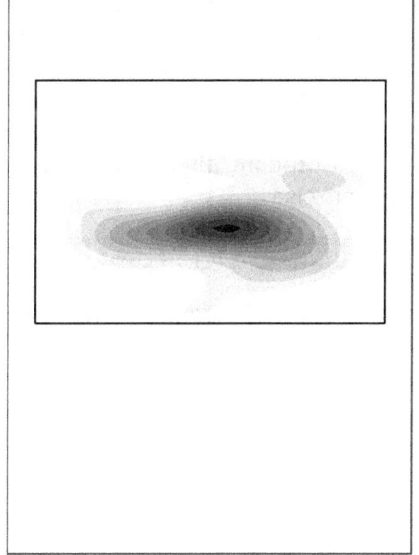

Matt Olson 1B

Born: 03/29/94   Age: 25   Bats: L   Throws: R
Height: 6'5"   Weight: 230   Origin: Round 1, 2012 Draft (#47 overall)

YEAR	TEAM	LVL	AGE	PA	R	2B	3B	HR	RBI	BB	K	SB	CS	AVG/OBP/SLG
2016	NAS	AAA	22	540	69	34	1	17	60	71	132	1	0	.235/.335/.422
2016	OAK	MLB	22	28	3	1	0	0	0	7	4	0	0	.095/.321/.143
2017	NAS	AAA	23	343	56	16	1	23	60	45	83	3	0	.272/.367/.568
2017	OAK	MLB	23	216	33	2	0	24	45	22	60	0	0	.259/.352/.651
2018	OAK	MLB	24	660	85	33	0	29	84	70	163	2	1	.247/.335/.453
2019	OAK	MLB	25	576	71	27	1	27	81	59	147	1	0	.226/.313/.443

Breakout: 13%   Improve: 56%   Collapse: 12%   Attrition: 9%   MLB: 97%
Comparables: Brandon Belt, Ike Davis, Paul Goldschmidt

So the 24:2 homers-to-doubles ratio from 2017 wasn't sustainable after all? Olson is a good illustration of what happens to first-base prospects: They can become perfectly fine major leaguers and very rarely end up anything special. That's even true when they win Gold Gloves, as Olson did last year with strong scoops and a good arm. The sorry state of first base in the American League means that Olson finished second in WARP at his position. Unsurprisingly for a player at his height, he did his best work on the low-and-away pitch, which he can golf out of the yard, but did absolutely nothing with offerings in the upper or inner thirds of the zone. Fortunately for him, even in a league in which the high pitch is ascendant, pitchers still worked more in the low-away quadrant than anywhere else.

YEAR	TEAM	LVL	AGE	PA	DRC+	VORP	BABIP	BRR	FRAA	WARP
2016	NAS	AAA	22	540	105	15.5	.289	-2.9	RF(81): -3.0, 1B(49): 3.9	0.1
2016	OAK	MLB	22	28	94	-1.6	.118	-0.2	RF(5): -0.7, 1B(4): -0.1	-0.1
2017	NAS	AAA	23	343	143	29.8	.298	-0.1	1B(73): -0.8, 3B(1): -0.2	1.6
2017	OAK	MLB	23	216	146	15.5	.238	0.3	1B(43): 4.7, RF(12): 2.7	2.4
2018	OAK	MLB	24	660	114	21.2	.292	-2.6	1B(162): 3.8	2.2
2019	OAK	MLB	25	576	109	17.2	.261	-1.1	1B 1	1.9

Matt Olson, continued

Batted Ball Distribution

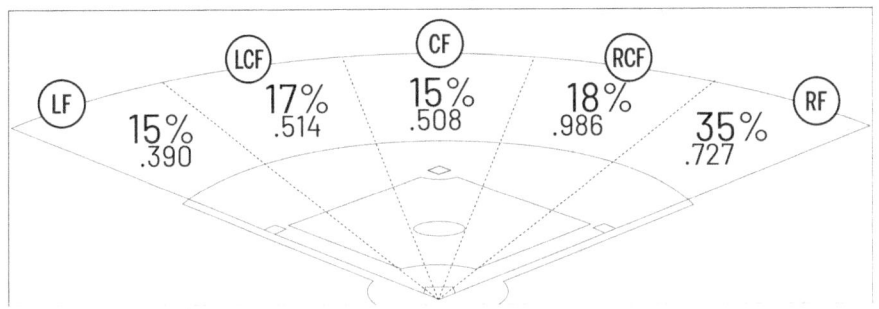

Strike Zone vs LHP

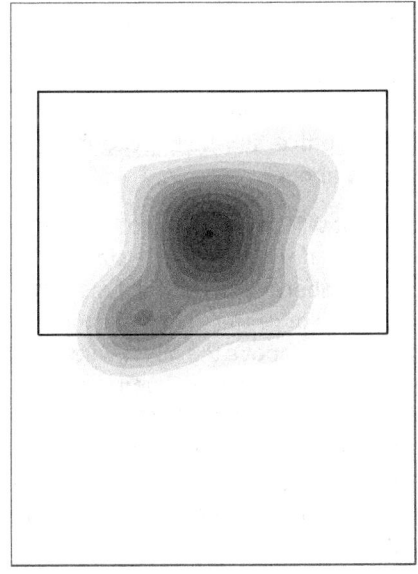

Strike Zone vs RHP

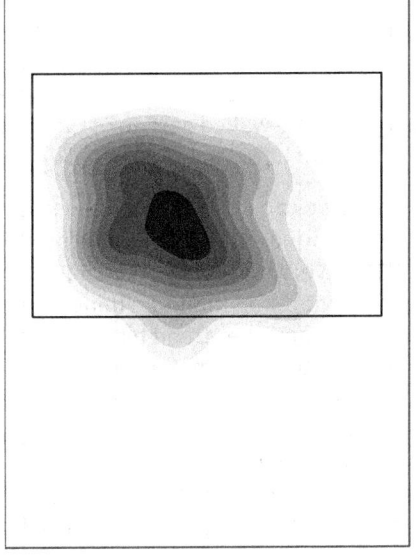

Chad Pinder UT

Born: 03/29/92 Age: 27 Bats: R Throws: R
Height: 6'2" Weight: 195 Origin: Round 2, 2013 Draft (#71 overall)

YEAR	TEAM	LVL	AGE	PA	R	2B	3B	HR	RBI	BB	K	SB	CS	AVG/OBP/SLG
2016	NAS	AAA	24	465	72	23	3	14	51	25	108	5	1	.258/.310/.425
2016	OAK	MLB	24	55	4	4	0	1	4	3	14	0	0	.235/.273/.373
2017	NAS	AAA	25	71	3	2	1	1	2	6	23	2	1	.266/.338/.375
2017	OAK	MLB	25	309	36	15	1	15	42	18	92	2	1	.238/.292/.457
2018	OAK	MLB	26	333	43	12	1	13	27	27	88	0	2	.258/.332/.436
2019	OAK	MLB	27	248	28	12	1	8	29	17	64	1	1	.244/.305/.413

Breakout: 7% Improve: 43% Collapse: 15% Attrition: 19% MLB: 88%
Comparables: Brennan Boesch, Cody Asche, Ryan Rua

In the 2000 edition of this book, Keith Woolner listed "quantifying the value of positional flexibility" as one of baseball's "Hilbert Problems," 23 critical areas for future research. Timothy C.Y. Chan and Douglas S. Fearing presented a paper at the 2013 MIT Sloan Sports Analytics Conference making inroads in this area by drawing on tools "from the theory of production flexibility in manufacturing networks," but this is hardly a solved problem in publicly available work, particularly at the individual level, and our own Russell A. Carleton has taken up on the cause in a series of recent articles. (Woolner himself has spent the last decade in the walled garden of Cleveland's front office, so who knows what kind of cool stuff he's figured out that we don't know about.)

What we can say with confidence is that extant WAR models do not account for the unique abilities of a player like Pinder, who drew at least one start in 2018 at every position but catcher, and did not embarrass himself defensively, even at shortstop (his main minor-league position) or center field. His cannon arm plays anywhere, and his overall batting line was above the MLB average at every position. He's not a starting-quality hitter against righties, even in the middle infield, but he'll run into enough homers against them that he doesn't need to immediately sit when the opposing team goes to its bullpen. Pinder isn't Tony Phillips, but he can absolutely be a winning team's 10th man. It's too bad he won't be eligible for free agency until 2023; it would be fascinating to see a player with this skill set hit the market with his powers intact.

YEAR	TEAM	LVL	AGE	PA	DRC+	VORP	BABIP	BRR	FRAA	WARP
2016	NAS	AAA	24	465	101	31.4	.312	4.5	SS(98): -4.2, 2B(4): -0.9	1.2
2016	OAK	MLB	24	55	81	0.4	.297	0.4	2B(13): 0.1, SS(7): -0.2	0.1
2017	NAS	AAA	25	71	75	0.7	.400	-1.5	2B(8): 0.1, SS(4): -0.3	-0.3
2017	OAK	MLB	25	309	97	6.9	.292	-1.8	RF(35): -0.5, SS(22): 1.6	0.8
2018	OAK	MLB	26	333	110	15.7	.325	0.8	LF(64): 4.8, 2B(21): -1.3	1.8
2019	OAK	MLB	27	248	94	5.6	.298	-0.4	3B 1, LF 1	0.6

Chad Pinder, continued

Batted Ball Distribution

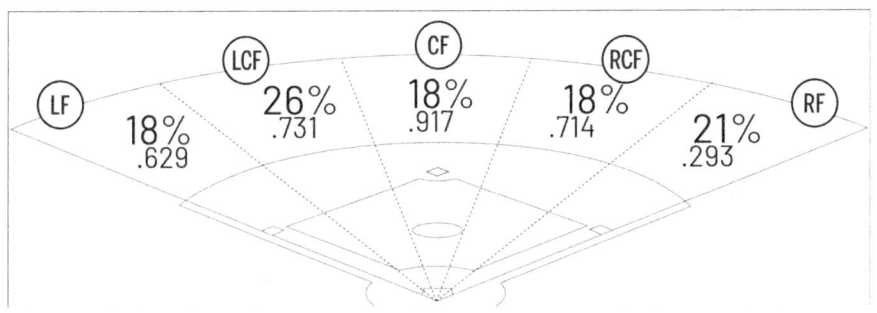

Strike Zone vs LHP   Strike Zone vs RHP

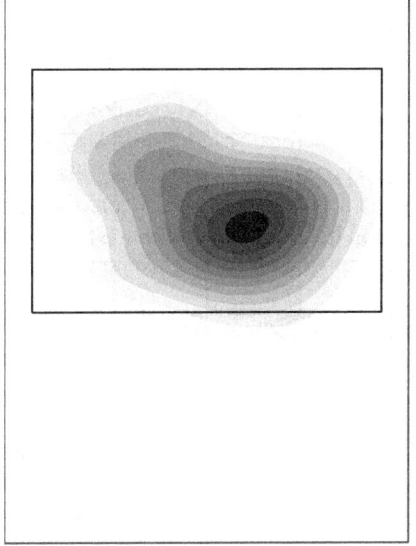

Stephen Piscotty RF

Born: 01/14/91   Age: 28   Bats: R   Throws: R
Height: 6'3"   Weight: 210   Origin: Round 1, 2012 Draft (#36 overall)

YEAR	TEAM	LVL	AGE	PA	R	2B	3B	HR	RBI	BB	K	SB	CS	AVG/OBP/SLG
2016	SLN	MLB	25	649	86	35	3	22	85	51	133	7	5	.273/.343/.457
2017	MEM	AAA	26	38	7	3	0	4	7	6	7	0	0	.313/.421/.781
2017	SLN	MLB	26	401	40	16	1	9	39	52	87	3	6	.235/.342/.367
2018	OAK	MLB	27	605	78	41	0	27	88	42	114	2	0	.267/.331/.491
2019	OAK	MLB	28	556	64	28	1	18	68	52	111	4	3	.252/.332/.423

Breakout: 2%   Improve: 47%   Collapse: 9%   Attrition: 19%   MLB: 95%
Comparables: Michael Saunders, Jeremy Hermida, Corey Hart

The Cardinals having their usual abundance of outfielders last winter allowed them to trade Piscotty to one of the two teams close enough to his hometown that he could spend his time off with his mother, Gretchen, who was in the late stages of a battle with ALS. She passed away in May, and one hopes that Piscotty's ability to spend April playing in Oakland rather than St. Louis gave him and his family some comfort in this difficult time. There remains some grace in the world.

On the field, physical health brought a welcome return to Piscotty's power stroke, though the early part of the season was rough, as you might imagine. His batting line bottomed out on May 27; from May 28 on, he hit .286/.352/.554, which is right around Jesus Aguilar's full-season figures. Even if you buy that he gave away nearly a win on defense, and even noting that he's now 28, the $28.5 million he's owed over the next four years looks like a bargain for a steady, "put him in the five hole and forget about him" right fielder.

YEAR	TEAM	LVL	AGE	PA	DRC+	VORP	BABIP	BRR	FRAA	WARP
2016	SLN	MLB	25	649	109	30.1	.319	-2.1	RF(146): -2.3, CF(10): 0.1	1.7
2017	MEM	AAA	26	38	186	6.9	.286	0.0	RF(6): -0.2	0.4
2017	SLN	MLB	26	401	95	1.6	.286	-2.5	RF(99): -0.9	0.3
2018	OAK	MLB	27	605	120	28.6	.290	-1.4	RF(151): -9.3	1.7
2019	OAK	MLB	28	556	110	21.5	.290	-1.3	RF -3	1.7

Stephen Piscotty, continued

Batted Ball Distribution

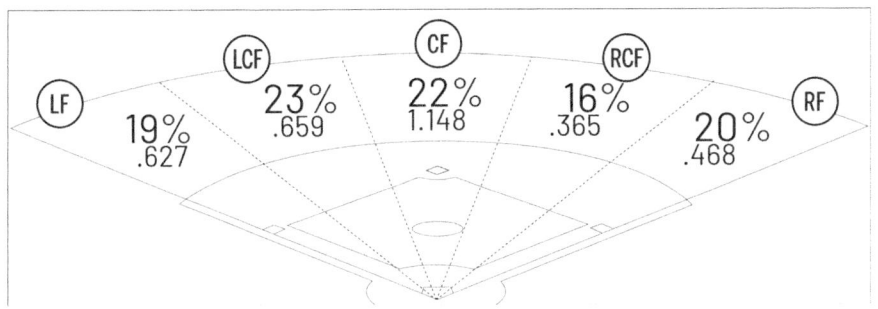

Strike Zone vs LHP

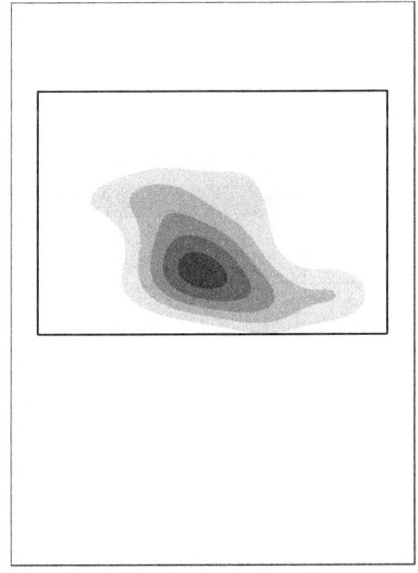

Strike Zone vs RHP

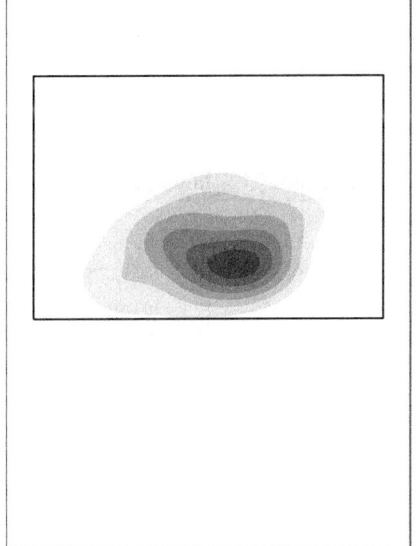

Jurickson Profar INF

Born: 02/20/93 Age: 26 Bats: B Throws: R
Height: 6'0" Weight: 190 Origin: International Free Agent, 2009

YEAR	TEAM	LVL	AGE	PA	R	2B	3B	HR	RBI	BB	K	SB	CS	AVG/OBP/SLG
2016	ROU	AAA	23	189	28	9	0	5	26	16	26	4	3	.284/.356/.426
2016	TEX	MLB	23	307	35	6	3	5	20	30	61	2	1	.239/.321/.338
2017	TEX	MLB	24	70	8	2	0	0	5	9	14	1	1	.172/.294/.207
2017	ROU	AAA	24	383	50	25	0	7	45	43	33	5	0	.287/.383/.428
2018	TEX	MLB	25	594	82	35	6	20	77	54	88	10	0	.254/.335/.458
2019	OAK	MLB	26	511	57	24	3	14	58	44	81	6	1	.249/.326/.408

Breakout: 5% Improve: 55% Collapse: 5% Attrition: 17% MLB: 99%
Comparables: Didi Gregorius, Enrique Hernandez, Brandon Crawford

It feels weird to write about Profar without using the word "prospect," but all traditions must eventually come to an end. Years lost to shoulder injuries and a slow return to the big leagues have dashed expectations that once projected Profar to be a baseball demigod, but a 20-homer season certainly allowed for hope that he's still an above-average regular. The end of Profar's prospectdom did not, however, mean the end of the trade rumors that have swirled around him for *checks notes* the last 72 years. Rather than fill the massive shoes of Adrian Beltre at third base in Texas, he'll replace Jed Lowrie at second base in Oakland.

YEAR	TEAM	LVL	AGE	PA	DRC+	VORP	BABIP	BRR	FRAA	WARP
2016	ROU	AAA	23	189	115	13.9	.312	0.2	SS(31): 2.9, 2B(6): 0.1	1.0
2016	TEX	MLB	23	307	82	-6.0	.291	-1.5	3B(25): -1.2, 2B(19): 1.9	0.0
2017	TEX	MLB	24	70	76	-0.8	.227	0.8	LF(12): 1.2, SS(4): -0.6	0.1
2017	ROU	AAA	24	383	119	32.9	.302	2.9	SS(78): -6.6, 2B(3): -0.2	1.7
2018	TEX	MLB	25	594	110	29.0	.269	2.2	SS(68): -8.6, 3B(51): -3.7	1.8
2019	OAK	MLB	26	511	100	17.7	.270	0.3	2B 7, 1B 1	2.4

Jurickson Profar, continued

Batted Ball Distribution

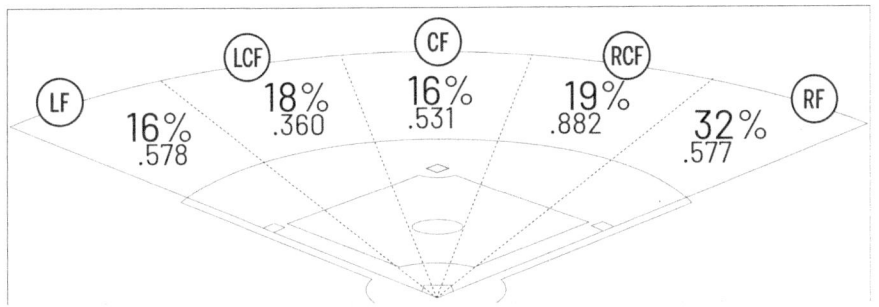

Strike Zone vs LHP

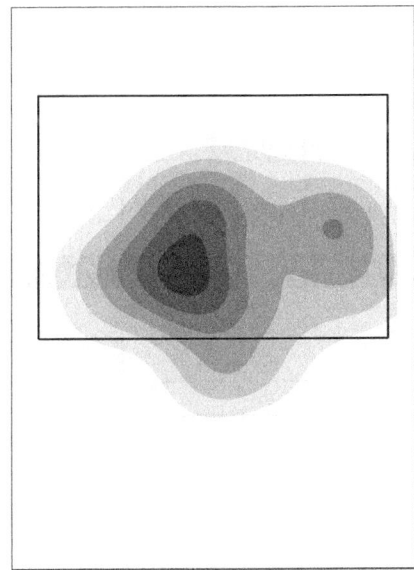

Strike Zone vs RHP

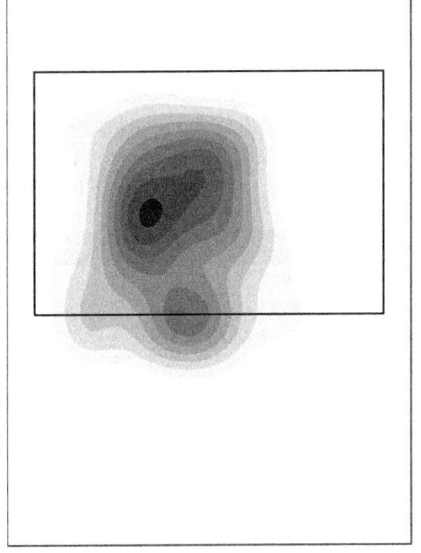

Athletics Player Analysis - 43

Marcus Semien SS

Born: 09/17/90 Age: 28 Bats: R Throws: R
Height: 6'0" Weight: 195 Origin: Round 6, 2011 Draft (#201 overall)

YEAR	TEAM	LVL	AGE	PA	R	2B	3B	HR	RBI	BB	K	SB	CS	AVG/OBP/SLG
2016	OAK	MLB	25	621	72	27	2	27	75	51	139	10	2	.238/.300/.435
2017	OAK	MLB	26	386	53	19	1	10	40	38	85	12	1	.249/.325/.398
2018	OAK	MLB	27	703	89	35	2	15	70	61	131	14	6	.255/.318/.388
2019	OAK	MLB	28	621	78	31	2	15	59	59	125	13	4	.245/.321/.390

Breakout: 6% Improve: 49% Collapse: 8% Attrition: 8% MLB: 97%
Comparables: Stephen Drew, Brandon Crawford, J.J. Hardy

Semien had a wrist injury in 2017 that some (okay, it was us) speculated might have led to his trade of slugging for on-base percentage. Last year, though, at apparent full health, he kept 2017's balance at the plate (making his 27-dinger 2016 look more like a spike than a skill), while allegedly adding defense to the equation. All the metrics agree that he provided substantial value with the glove last year, though the enormous jump compared to years past is hard to swallow without any obvious physical changes. There's this, though: Semien was positioned more up the middle than any MLB shortstop except for Houston's trio. (Data from Semien's prior three years shows him in a league-average spot.) It's hard not to attribute this change to Matt Chapman playing every day a few feet to Semien's right. Even without the defense, though, Semien is probably the best shortstop whose name is never spoken outside of his team's fan base. But hey, it's an honor just to be invited and all that, right?

YEAR	TEAM	LVL	AGE	PA	DRC+	VORP	BABIP	BRR	FRAA	WARP
2016	OAK	MLB	25	621	107	32.2	.268	2.6	SS(159): 1.0	3.7
2017	OAK	MLB	26	386	94	18.2	.300	3.9	SS(85): -1.5	1.7
2018	OAK	MLB	27	703	99	38.0	.296	5.4	SS(159): 16.2	5.4
2019	OAK	MLB	28	621	96	25.7	.290	0.5	SS 5	2.6

Marcus Semien, continued

Batted Ball Distribution

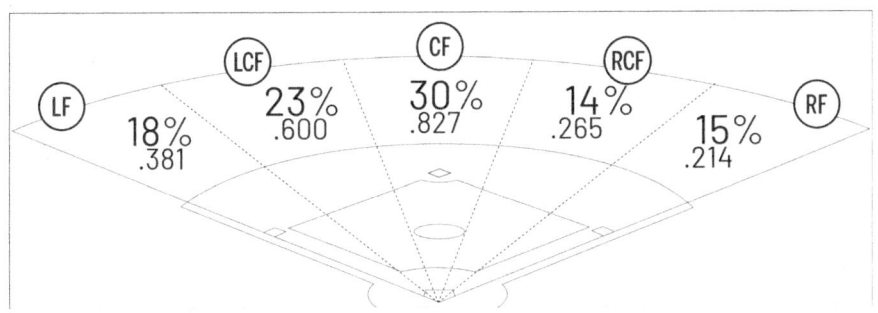

Strike Zone vs LHP   **Strike Zone vs RHP**

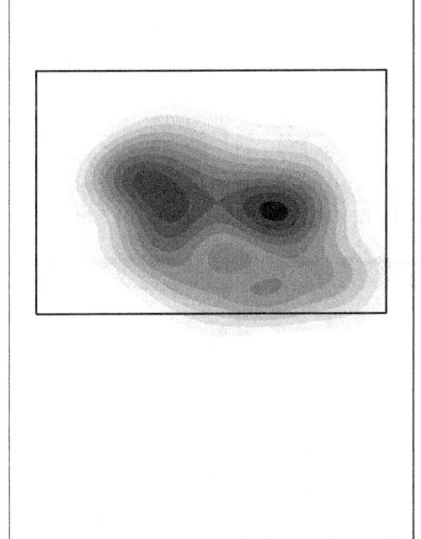

Brett Anderson LHP

Born: 02/01/88 Age: 31 Bats: L Throws: L
Height: 6'3" Weight: 230 Origin: Round 2, 2006 Draft (#55 overall)

YEAR	TEAM	LVL	AGE	W	L	SV	G	GS	IP	H	HR	BB/9	K/9	K	GB%	BABIP
2016	LAN	MLB	28	1	2	0	4	3	11^1	25	4	3.2	4.0	5	51%	.429
2017	CHN	MLB	29	2	2	0	6	6	22	34	2	4.9	6.5	16	51%	.395
2017	TEN	AA	29	2	2	0	6	5	27^1	34	2	3.0	4.9	15	69%	.348
2017	BUF	AAA	29	1	1	0	2	2	9^2	4	0	1.9	2.8	3	53%	.133
2017	TOR	MLB	29	2	2	0	7	7	33^1	39	3	2.4	5.9	22	50%	.340
2018	NAS	AAA	30	2	1	0	7	7	32^1	32	0	1.7	10.0	36	60%	.333
2018	OAK	MLB	30	4	5	0	17	17	80^1	90	10	1.5	5.3	47	57%	.307
2019	OAK	MLB	31	4	5	0	15	15	70	75	9	3.0	6.3	49	51%	.299

Breakout: 22%   Improve: 44%   Collapse: 18%   Attrition: 13%   MLB: 76%
Comparables: Tommy John, Andy Pettitte, Dillon Gee

Anderson was once a tantalizing talent you'd employ with the expectation of injury and the hope for high-quality innings when healthy. If you had some money to burn and a good sixth man waiting in Triple-A, he could provide value. Now? With a 5.76 ERA over his last three seasons? While averaging well under five innings per start and throwing his fastball 90-92? Now it's hard to imagine another major-league contract for as long as he wants to hang on. (And if he signed one between the time we went to press and the time you read this, well, you know where to yell at us.) After he got absolutely pasted in the posterior by a 110 mph liner off the bat of Shohei Ohtani in his last start of the year, it's worth asking just how much longer Anderson wants that to be.

YEAR	TEAM	LVL	AGE	WHIP	ERA	DRA	WARP	MPH	FB%	WHF	CSP
2016	LAN	MLB	28	2.56	11.91	6.83	-0.2	94.2	58.7	5.8	47
2017	CHN	MLB	29	2.09	8.18	4.87	0.2	92.2	56.7	9	41.6
2017	TEN	AA	29	1.57	4.61	4.37	0.2				
2017	BUF	AAA	29	0.62	0.93	4.18	0.2				
2017	TOR	MLB	29	1.44	5.13	5.88	-0.1	93.2	48.6	9.5	46.3
2018	NAS	AAA	30	1.18	2.78	3.21	0.9				
2018	OAK	MLB	30	1.28	4.48	3.98	1.2	92.6	49.5	8.1	49.2
2019	OAK	MLB	31	1.42	4.37	4.97	0.4	91.9	50.7	8.3	46.7

Brett Anderson, continued

Pitch Shape vs LHH

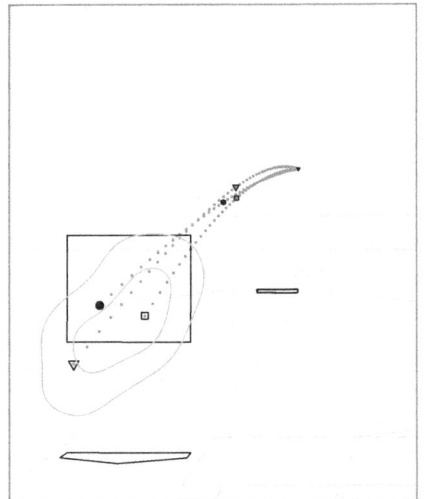

Pitch Shape vs RHH

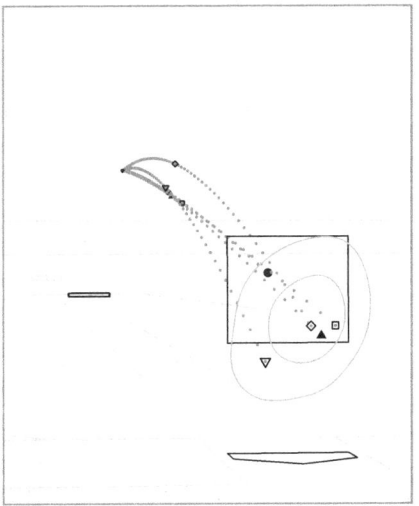

Type	Frequency	Velocity	H Movement	V Movement
● Fastball	18.2%	91.6 [97]	6.4 [101]	-15.8 [100]
☐ Sinker	31.3%	90.4 [90]	12.8 [98]	-20.9 [98]
+ Cutter				
▲ Changeup	18.9%	83.9 [94]	13.1 [90]	-27.1 [101]
✕ Splitter				
▽ Slider	24.9%	82.6 [92]	-2 [88]	-43.1 [70]
◇ Curveball	6.7%	76.4 [92]	-4.7 [87]	-55.1 [84]
⊕ Slow Curveball				
✳ Knuckleball				
▼ Screwball				

Chris Bassitt RHP

Born: 02/22/89 Age: 30 Bats: R Throws: R
Height: 6'5" Weight: 220 Origin: Round 16, 2011 Draft (#501 overall)

YEAR	TEAM	LVL	AGE	W	L	SV	G	GS	IP	H	HR	BB/9	K/9	K	GB%	BABIP
2016	OAK	MLB	27	0	2	0	5	5	28	35	5	4.5	7.4	23	47%	.330
2017	STO	A+	28	0	1	0	7	7	13	9	0	2.8	9.7	14	64%	.273
2017	NAS	AAA	28	4	2	0	17	2	37²	41	3	3.8	7.4	31	36%	.336
2018	NAS	AAA	29	5	5	0	18	14	81²	86	6	2.8	9.1	83	44%	.348
2018	OAK	MLB	29	2	3	0	11	7	47²	40	4	3.6	7.7	41	44%	.265
2019	OAK	MLB	30	2	2	0	17	5	39	39	5	3.6	7.6	33	43%	.293

Breakout: 19% Improve: 33% Collapse: 16% Attrition: 12% MLB: 58%
Comparables: Clay Hensley, Christian Friedrich, Chris Heston

In his first full season back from a mid-2016 Tommy John surgery, Bassitt was optioned to Triple-A no fewer than seven times. It was his final option year, so props to the A's for making the most of it? (Two of his seven recalls resulted in no game action, so maybe it depends on your definition of "the most of it.") Bassitt's official stats show seven starts, but that omits three games pitching behind "opener" Liam Hendriks in September. He struck out 11 in 10 innings in those games, but the A's left him off their Wild Card game roster despite taking 10 relief pitchers (plus Edwin Jackson) to New York. All of that, plus stuff that simply isn't impressive in 2018 (much as the 20 mph differential between his fastball and curve is fun), spells a lot of "designated for assignment" in his future.

YEAR	TEAM	LVL	AGE	WHIP	ERA	DRA	WARP	MPH	FB%	WHF	CSP
2016	OAK	MLB	27	1.75	6.11	5.96	-0.2	96.0	59.2	9	49.7
2017	STO	A+	28	1.00	2.77	3.65	0.2				
2017	NAS	AAA	28	1.51	6.21	4.53	0.4				
2018	NAS	AAA	29	1.36	4.30	3.80	1.5				
2018	OAK	MLB	29	1.24	3.02	5.24	0.0	94.2	57.4	7.6	51.8
2019	OAK	MLB	30	1.38	4.58	5.07	0.1	93.9	57.7	7.9	50.9

Chris Bassitt, continued

Pitch Shape vs LHH

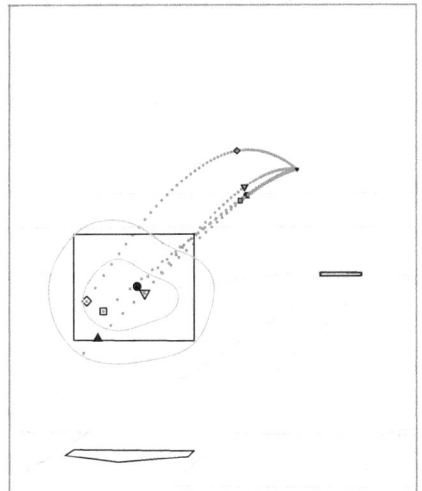

Pitch Shape vs RHH

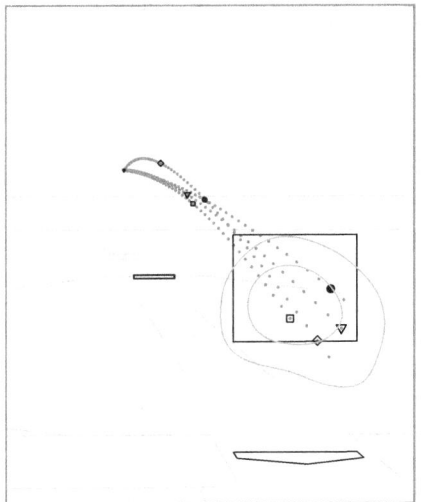

Type	Frequency	Velocity	H Movement	V Movement
● Fastball	13.3%	92.8 [101]	-6.1 [103]	-16 [99]
□ Sinker	44.1%	92.3 [99]	-13.1 [96]	-19.4 [103]
+ Cutter				
▲ Changeup	4.3%	83.3 [92]	-13.6 [88]	-28.1 [98]
× Splitter				
▽ Slider	25.0%	86.9 [111]	3.6 [94]	-25.8 [121]
◇ Curveball	13.3%	71.4 [74]	12.8 [121]	-60 [73]
✦ Slow Curveball				
✳ Knuckleball				
▼ Screwball				

Jerry Blevins LHP
Born: 09/06/83   Age: 35   Bats: L   Throws: L
Height: 6'6"   Weight: 190   Origin: Round 17, 2004 Draft (#516 overall)

YEAR	TEAM	LVL	AGE	W	L	SV	G	GS	IP	H	HR	BB/9	K/9	K	GB%	BABIP
2016	NYN	MLB	32	4	2	2	73	0	42	36	4	3.2	11.1	52	47%	.302
2017	NYN	MLB	33	6	0	1	75	0	49	43	4	4.4	12.7	69	42%	.336
2018	NYN	MLB	34	3	2	1	64	1	42²	36	6	4.6	8.6	41	22%	.263
2019	OAK	MLB	35	2	1	1	36	0	38¹	34	6	4.2	9.1	39	36%	.275

Breakout: 20%   Improve: 37%   Collapse: 29%   Attrition: 19%   MLB: 86%
Comparables: Kerry Wood, George Sherrill, Damaso Marte

For four seasons Blevins was a surprisingly steady and effective left-handed relief option, but he sure picked the wrong time to have his first bad season in a half-decade. This veteran southpaw went from bullpen lynchpin to two steps ahead of the lynch mob despite little change to his repertoire or velocity. His signature fastball lost some horizontal movement and hitters put it in the air much more than usual, but the underlying speed of the pitch never changed (except as it reverberated off left hitters' bats). And despite being asked to face more right-handed hitters than usual, it was the lefties who surprisingly beat up on him when he couldn't get swings and misses. He'll now go into his age-35 season bereft of contract and looking to make good rather than make bank. There's reason to think he'll rebound, but the damage to his wallet has been done.

YEAR	TEAM	LVL	AGE	WHIP	ERA	DRA	WARP	MPH	FB%	WHF	CSP
2016	NYN	MLB	32	1.21	2.79	2.53	1.2	91.5	62.5	11.5	47.2
2017	NYN	MLB	33	1.37	2.94	2.94	1.2	90.4	45.7	13.2	39
2018	NYN	MLB	34	1.36	4.85	7.12	-1.1	90.4	51.7	9.6	47
2019	OAK	MLB	35	1.36	4.93	5.44	-0.1	89.5	50.9	11.2	43.6

Jerry Blevins, continued

Pitch Shape vs LHH

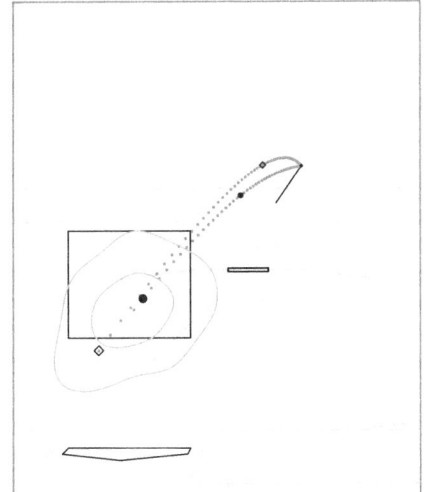

Pitch Shape vs RHH

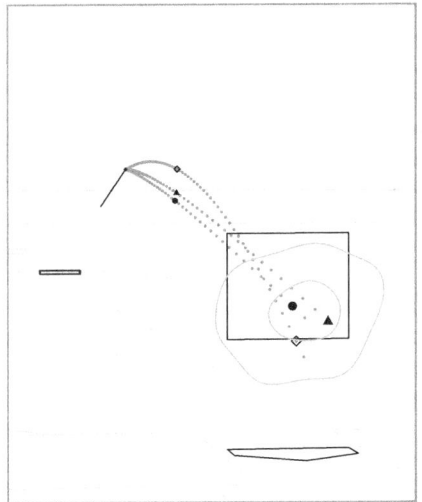

Type	Frequency	Velocity	H Movement	V Movement
● Fastball	51.7%	89.3 [90]	7.6 [96]	-16.9 [96]
☐ Sinker				
+ Cutter				
▲ Changeup	8.5%	83.7 [93]	12.1 [95]	-26.1 [104]
× Splitter				
▽ Slider				
◇ Curveball	39.8%	72.6 [78]	-12.2 [118]	-53.6 [88]
⊕ Slow Curveball				
✳ Knuckleball				
▼ Screwball				

Ryan Buchter   LHP

Born: 02/13/87   Age: 32   Bats: L   Throws: L
Height: 6'4"   Weight: 258   Origin: Round 33, 2005 Draft (#984 overall)

YEAR	TEAM	LVL	AGE	W	L	SV	G	GS	IP	H	HR	BB/9	K/9	K	GB%	BABIP
2016	SDN	MLB	29	3	0	1	67	0	63	34	4	4.4	11.1	78	21%	.227
2017	SDN	MLB	30	3	3	1	42	0	38¹	28	7	4.2	11.0	47	33%	.239
2017	KCA	MLB	30	1	0	0	29	0	27	16	3	2.7	6.0	18	32%	.173
2018	OAK	MLB	31	6	0	0	54	0	39¹	32	4	3.4	9.4	41	28%	.272
2019	OAK	MLB	32	3	3	0	54	0	57	50	9	4.1	9.0	57	32%	.276

Breakout: 25%   Improve: 46%   Collapse: 17%   Attrition: 17%   MLB: 75%
Comparables: Al Alburquerque, Cory Gearrin, Louis Coleman

The A's picked Buchter up in a scrap-heap swap with the Royals that also saw Brandon Moss moving to Oakland in exchange for Heath Fillmyer and Jesse Hahn. Buchter spent the year as Oakland's main bullpen lefty (outside of a six-week stint on the DL with a shoulder strain), facing 92 same-side hitters against just 71 righties. He reincorporated a cutter and curve that he'd all but eliminated in 2016 and 2017, but the outcomes were essentially the same: solid strikeout numbers, scads of fly balls (and therefore more dong shots than you'd like) and something less than pinpoint control. Remember the old "if he could just cut one walk per nine while keeping everything else the same …" game? Buchter did it, at least for 163 batters last year, and thereby made himself an employable big-league relief pitcher. On the one hand, that's right around the size of sample in which you can feel a little bit of confidence; on the other, he's spent the six months since he last pitched getting older, just like the rest of us. Go ahead and scribble his name in as your middle-relief lefty this year, but have a backup plan.

YEAR	TEAM	LVL	AGE	WHIP	ERA	DRA	WARP	MPH	FB%	WHF	CSP
2016	SDN	MLB	29	1.03	2.86	5.61	-0.5	94.6	84.7	10.8	45.5
2017	SDN	MLB	30	1.20	3.05	5.03	0.1	94.3	72.1	12.7	47.3
2017	KCA	MLB	30	0.89	2.67	5.67	-0.2	94.0	72.1	10.3	49.8
2018	OAK	MLB	31	1.19	2.75	3.60	0.6	94.0	65.7	12.2	48.1
2019	OAK	MLB	32	1.31	4.84	5.13	0.0	93.3	73.2	11.5	47.1

Ryan Buchter, continued

Pitch Shape vs LHH

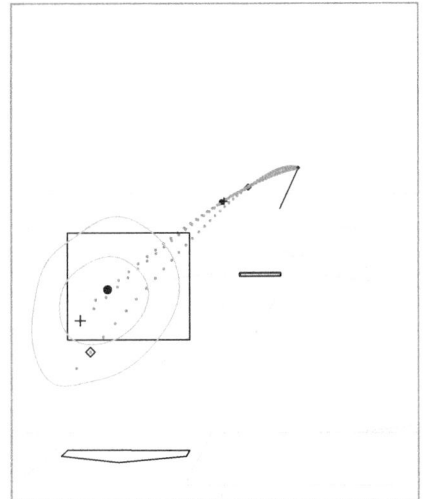

Pitch Shape vs RHH

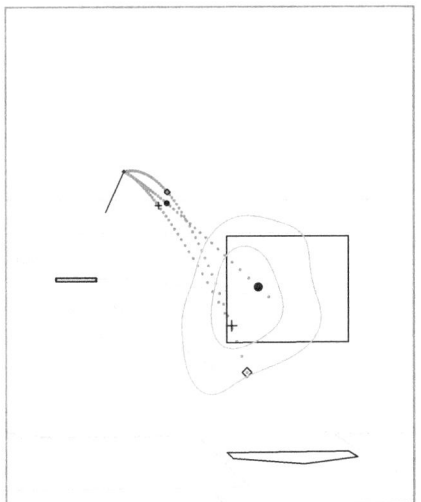

Type	Frequency	Velocity	H Movement	V Movement
● Fastball	65.7%	93.2 [102]	7.2 [98]	-12 [112]
☐ Sinker				
+ Cutter	17.4%	90.1 [108]	1.2 [82]	-19 [119]
▲ Changeup				
✕ Splitter				
▽ Slider	2.5%	81.7 [87]	-8.7 [117]	-34.6 [95]
◇ Curveball	14.4%	79.9 [105]	-11.6 [116]	-39.1 [120]
⊕ Slow Curveball				
✳ Knuckleball				
▼ Screwball				

Marco Estrada   RHP
Born: 07/05/83   Age: 35   Bats: R   Throws: R
Height: 6'0"   Weight: 180   Origin: Round 6, 2005 Draft (#174 overall)

YEAR	TEAM	LVL	AGE	W	L	SV	G	GS	IP	H	HR	BB/9	K/9	K	GB%	BABIP
2016	TOR	MLB	32	9	9	0	29	29	176	132	23	3.3	8.4	165	35%	.234
2017	TOR	MLB	33	10	9	0	33	33	186	186	31	3.4	8.5	176	31%	.295
2018	TOR	MLB	34	7	14	0	28	28	143²	155	29	3.1	6.5	103	26%	.285
2019	OAK	MLB	35	7	10	0	24	24	127	132	27	3.2	6.6	94	32%	.276

Breakout: 15%   Improve: 33%   Collapse: 27%   Attrition: 10%   MLB: 86%
Comparables: Earl Wilson, Bruce Hurst, Jason Hammel

You can say three definitive things about Estrada. First: His changeup—the singular force driving his career resurgence since 2015—is failing. He threw it more than ever in 2018, favoring the slow, hovering pitch over a fastball that barely crested 89 mph and a handful of secondaries that became fodder for the second-highest home run rate in the league yet batters rocked it for a .248 average and .281 BABIP even so. Second: His diligence to his craft is taking an irreversible toll on his body. After getting diagnosed with a left glute strain in July, he attempted to pitch through a painful bulging disc and arthritic joints in his back, conditions that, when combined, forced him to limp into free agency. Third: There's nowhere for the slow-tossing righty to go but up. Estrada may not be capable of another award-worthy transformation in his age-35 season, but as anyone who's tried (and failed) to anticipate the erratic backspin of his signature pitch can tell you, he's never been one to look for success in all the conventional places, either.

YEAR	TEAM	LVL	AGE	WHIP	ERA	DRA	WARP	MPH	FB%	WHF	CSP
2016	TOR	MLB	32	1.12	3.48	4.30	2.1	90.2	50.1	12	44.8
2017	TOR	MLB	33	1.38	4.98	5.76	-0.4	91.0	53.8	11.8	47.4
2018	TOR	MLB	34	1.43	5.64	7.16	-3.1	90.0	49.2	11.3	46.3
2019	OAK	MLB	35	1.35	5.53	6.24	-1.2	89.3	50.3	11.5	45.5

Marco Estrada, continued

Pitch Shape vs LHH

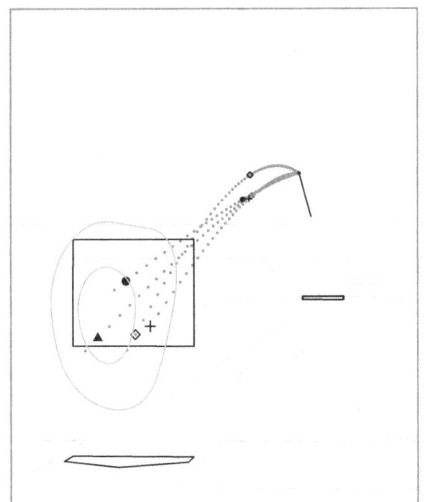

Pitch Shape vs RHH

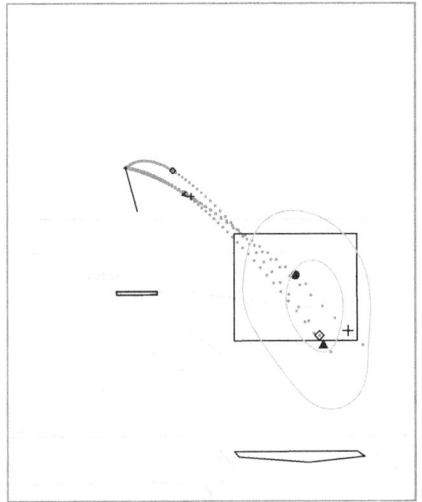

Type	Frequency	Velocity	H Movement	V Movement
● Fastball	49.2%	89 [89]	-3.2 [116]	-12 [112]
☐ Sinker				
+ Cutter	6.1%	85.4 [80]	4.5 [115]	-25.4 [93]
▲ Changeup	37.0%	77.2 [68]	-8.1 [117]	-25.4 [106]
✕ Splitter				
▽ Slider				
◇ Curveball	7.7%	76.9 [94]	5.1 [89]	-50.3 [95]
✦ Slow Curveball				
✳ Knuckleball				
▼ Screwball				

Mike Fiers RHP

Born: 06/15/85 Age: 34 Bats: R Throws: R
Height: 6'2" Weight: 202 Origin: Round 22, 2009 Draft (#676 overall)

YEAR	TEAM	LVL	AGE	W	L	SV	G	GS	IP	H	HR	BB/9	K/9	K	GB%	BABIP
2016	HOU	MLB	31	11	8	0	31	30	168²	187	26	2.2	7.2	134	44%	.313
2017	HOU	MLB	32	8	10	0	29	28	153¹	157	32	3.6	8.6	146	43%	.300
2018	DET	MLB	33	7	6	0	21	21	119	121	20	2.0	6.6	87	39%	.277
2018	OAK	MLB	33	5	2	0	10	9	53	45	12	1.9	8.8	52	43%	.246
2019	OAK	MLB	34	9	10	0	27	27	153	156	25	2.6	7.1	122	42%	.287

Breakout: 20% Improve: 44% Collapse: 18% Attrition: 8% MLB: 86%
Comparables: Chris Capuano, Ben Sheets, Jake Peavy

The A's didn't start the Fiers in the playoffs after a disastrous final game in the regular season when he followed an "opener" for the first time and got lit up for six runs in three-plus innings. Fiers had been a huge part of Oakland's burning-hot push to October, pitching in eight wins to just one loss, allowing two runs or fewer in seven of those eight. But since the world's been turning, pitchers with this kind of profile tend to fall off cliffs: He lives on low-velocity fastballs up in the zone and therefore gives up a ton of loud contact and fly balls, with one result being 90 dingers allowed over the last three years, second only to James Shields. PECOTA isn't buying the 2018 semi-resurgence at all, but the A's bought in for a two-year, $14 million deal, bringing back Fiers after initially non-tendering him.

YEAR	TEAM	LVL	AGE	WHIP	ERA	DRA	WARP	MPH	FB%	WHF	CSP
2016	HOU	MLB	31	1.36	4.48	4.46	1.7	91.9	41.1	9.9	46.7
2017	HOU	MLB	32	1.43	5.22	5.82	-0.4	91.5	47.5	9.9	46.6
2018	DET	MLB	33	1.24	3.48	4.87	0.6	91.2	46.7	8.8	49.1
2018	OAK	MLB	33	1.06	3.74	4.02	0.8	91.9	46.7	10.1	50.9
2019	OAK	MLB	34	1.29	4.61	5.21	0.4	90.5	44.9	9.5	47.2

Mike Fiers, continued

Pitch Shape vs LHH

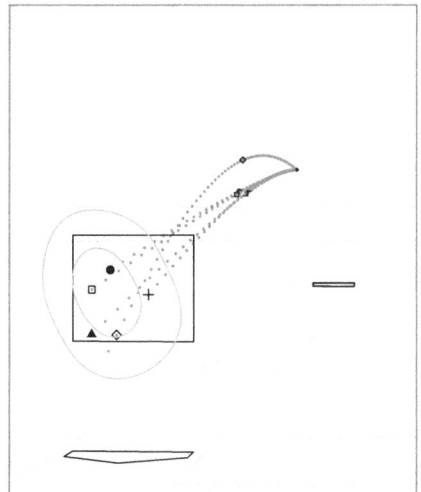

Pitch Shape vs RHH

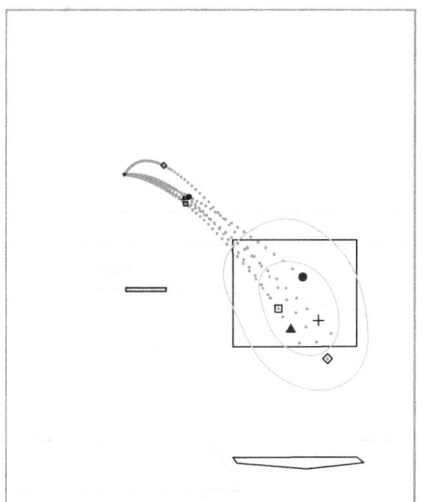

Type		Frequency	Velocity	H Movement	V Movement
●	Fastball	34.9%	90 [92]	-6.4 [101]	-13.6 [107]
□	Sinker	13.2%	89.7 [86]	-11.3 [111]	-17.5 [109]
+	Cutter	16.8%	86 [84]	1.4 [97]	-23 [103]
▲	Changeup	18.2%	83.8 [94]	-12.8 [92]	-28.9 [95]
×	Splitter				
▽	Slider	1.0%	82.7 [92]	4.9 [100]	-30 [109]
◇	Curveball	15.8%	72.9 [79]	10.7 [112]	-63.4 [65]
⊕	Slow Curveball				
✳	Knuckleball				
▼	Screwball				

Daniel Gossett RHP

Born: 11/13/92 Age: 26 Bats: R Throws: R
Height: 6'2" Weight: 185 Origin: Round 2, 2014 Draft (#65 overall)

YEAR	TEAM	LVL	AGE	W	L	SV	G	GS	IP	H	HR	BB/9	K/9	K	GB%	BABIP
2016	STO	A+	23	4	1	0	9	9	46	40	4	2.5	10.4	53	54%	.295
2016	MID	AA	23	5	5	0	16	16	94	75	4	2.4	9.0	94	59%	.284
2016	NAS	AAA	23	1	0	0	2	2	13^2	10	0	2.0	2.6	4	57%	.227
2017	NAS	AAA	24	4	4	0	14	14	76^1	70	6	2.8	8.4	71	52%	.292
2017	OAK	MLB	24	4	11	0	18	18	91^1	116	21	3.1	7.1	72	45%	.328
2018	NAS	AAA	25	4	0	0	7	5	38^2	26	1	3.7	9.8	42	50%	.260
2018	OAK	MLB	25	0	3	0	5	5	24^1	25	5	3.0	4.4	12	42%	.263
2019	OAK	MLB	26	4	4	0	13	13	71	62	8	3.3	8.1	64	47%	.274

Breakout: 25% Improve: 44% Collapse: 20% Attrition: 37% MLB: 78%
Comparables: J.R. Graham, Luis Cessa, John Lamb

The A's lost a bunch of starting pitchers to injury in 2018, from top prospect A.J. Puk to solid starters Kendall Graveman and Sean Manaea to young guy with upside Jharel Cotton to ... well, what is Gossett, exactly? You want to say "don't judge a guy by his performance in a season when he winds up needing Tommy John surgery" but then you realize he pitched just fine in Triple-A. So maybe Gossett simply isn't a big-league starter. He didn't have his surgery until August, so there's no reason to expect him back until 2020. Don't be surprised if the A's, or whichever team he's on by that point, try him out of the bullpen to see if he can add a few feet to his fastball and avoid the pounding that has typified his career to this point.

YEAR	TEAM	LVL	AGE	WHIP	ERA	DRA	WARP	MPH	FB%	WHF	CSP
2016	STO	A+	23	1.15	3.33	2.42	1.6				
2016	MID	AA	23	1.06	2.49	3.02	2.3				
2016	NAS	AAA	23	0.95	1.98	3.30	0.3				
2017	NAS	AAA	24	1.23	3.66	3.35	2.0				
2017	OAK	MLB	24	1.61	6.11	5.76	-0.2	93.0	52.9	9.6	47.5
2018	NAS	AAA	25	1.09	1.63	2.34	1.3				
2018	OAK	MLB	25	1.36	5.18	5.05	0.1	94.5	51.4	8.7	51
2019	OAK	MLB	26	1.24	4.16	4.60	0.7	93.0	53.5	9.6	50.3

Daniel Gossett, continued

Pitch Shape vs LHH

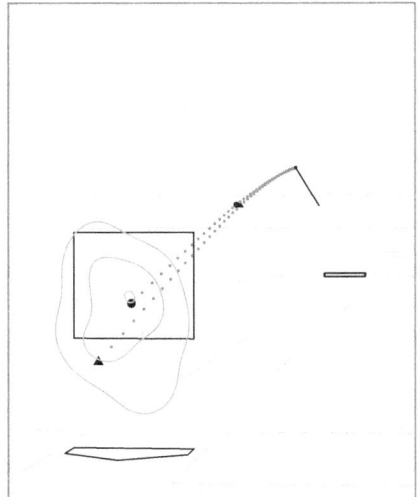

Pitch Shape vs RHH

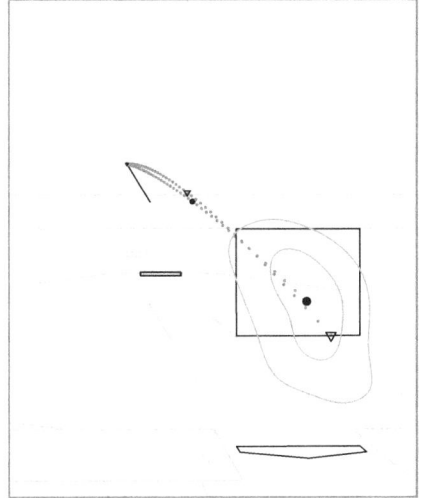

Type	Frequency	Velocity	H Movement	V Movement
● Fastball	42.2%	94 [105]	-0.9 [127]	-13.3 [108]
□ Sinker	9.3%	94 [108]	-10.7 [116]	-14.9 [118]
+ Cutter				
▲ Changeup	9.8%	86.3 [104]	-7.7 [119]	-24.6 [108]
× Splitter				
▽ Slider	29.8%	87.7 [115]	5.6 [103]	-29.6 [110]
◇ Curveball	9.0%	81.4 [111]	6.3 [94]	-44 [109]
⊕ Slow Curveball				
✻ Knuckleball				
▼ Screwball				

Liam Hendriks RHP

Born: 02/10/89 Age: 30 Bats: R Throws: R
Height: 6'0" Weight: 200 Origin: International Free Agent, 2007

YEAR	TEAM	LVL	AGE	W	L	SV	G	GS	IP	H	HR	BB/9	K/9	K	GB%	BABIP
2016	OAK	MLB	27	0	4	0	53	0	64²	69	6	1.9	9.9	71	42%	.344
2017	OAK	MLB	28	4	2	1	70	0	64	57	7	3.2	11.0	78	41%	.303
2018	NAS	AAA	29	4	1	6	23	1	25¹	21	1	1.4	15.3	43	41%	.364
2018	OAK	MLB	29	0	1	0	25	8	24	25	3	3.8	8.2	22	41%	.324
2019	OAK	MLB	30	3	3	0	50	8	57	52	6	3.2	9.8	63	41%	.298

Breakout: 25%   Improve: 50%   Collapse: 18%   Attrition: 15%   MLB: 83%
Comparables: Kevin Gregg, Adam Ottavino, Tony Watson

Meet your 2018 A's Wild Card game starter. Faced with injury after injury to what was a mediocre starting staff even at full health, Oakland decided to emulate the Rays and build the whole plane out of the black box, adding reliever after reliever to the roster in trades and trying out the "opener" thing in September. The maneuver was something of an obvious one, considering their other options, but the choice of personnel was substantially less obvious: Hendriks was designated for assignment in June and went unclaimed on waivers, leading to an outright assignment to Triple-A. He returned to the majors only when rosters expanded in September. Because of Bob Melvin's weird magic touch, Hendriks proceeded to post a 1.38 ERA in 13 September innings, salvaging his season. After all the noise, though, Hendriks is a 30-year-old middle reliever who throws hard but gives up a lot of fly balls, which is the same thing he was in 2018 (except he was 29 that year) and 2017 (28) and 2016 (27). Expect more of the same, which for Hendriks always includes the possibility of a bad three weeks when he allows four homers and gets cut.

YEAR	TEAM	LVL	AGE	WHIP	ERA	DRA	WARP	MPH	FB%	WHF	CSP
2016	OAK	MLB	27	1.28	3.76	3.89	0.8	96.8	75.6	12.5	50.7
2017	OAK	MLB	28	1.25	4.22	3.45	1.2	96.3	74.1	13.6	46.7
2018	NAS	AAA	29	0.99	2.84	2.31	0.8				
2018	OAK	MLB	29	1.46	4.12	4.70	0.1	97.2	70.1	12.1	47.1
2019	OAK	MLB	30	1.25	3.40	3.94	0.9	95.9	73.5	12.9	47.7

Liam Hendriks, continued

Pitch Shape vs LHH

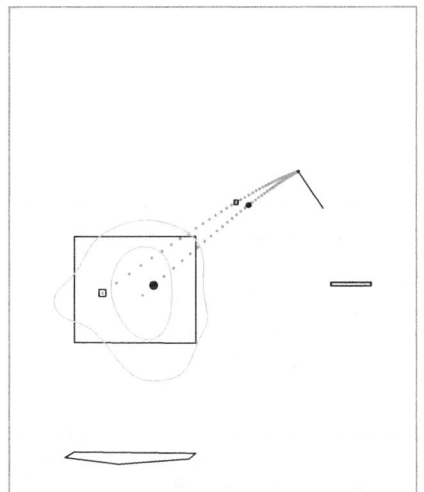

Pitch Shape vs RHH

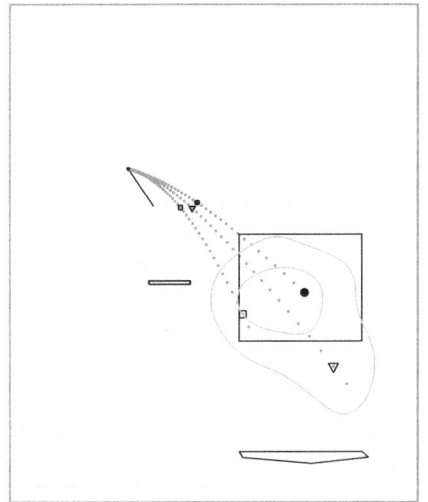

Type	Frequency	Velocity	H Movement	V Movement
● Fastball	48.3%	95.4 [109]	-6.1 [103]	-11.2 [115]
☐ Sinker	21.8%	93.9 [107]	-10.9 [114]	-15.3 [117]
+ Cutter				
▲ Changeup	1.6%	88.7 [113]	-10.4 [104]	-19.6 [123]
✕ Splitter				
▽ Slider	26.5%	87.2 [112]	3.8 [95]	-28.3 [114]
◇ Curveball	1.8%	82.8 [116]	1.4 [73]	-40.5 [117]
⊕ Slow Curveball				
✱ Knuckleball				
▼ Screwball				

Athletics Player Analysis - 61

Sean Manaea   LHP
Born: 02/01/92   Age: 27   Bats: R   Throws: L
Height: 6'5"   Weight: 245   Origin: Round 1, 2013 Draft (#34 overall)

YEAR	TEAM	LVL	AGE	W	L	SV	G	GS	IP	H	HR	BB/9	K/9	K	GB%	BABIP
2016	NAS	AAA	24	2	0	0	3	3	18	16	1	2.0	10.5	21	54%	.319
2016	OAK	MLB	24	7	9	0	25	24	144²	135	20	2.3	7.7	124	46%	.281
2017	OAK	MLB	25	12	10	0	29	29	158²	167	18	3.1	7.9	140	44%	.318
2018	OAK	MLB	26	12	9	0	27	27	160²	141	21	1.8	6.0	108	46%	.247
2019	OAK	MLB	27	1	1	0	3	3	15	15	2	2.6	7.2	12	45%	.293

Breakout: 23%   Improve: 57%   Collapse: 12%   Attrition: 9%   MLB: 90%
Comparables: Manny Parra, Paul Maholm, Brett Anderson

Manaea had a very solid mid-rotation season, with fewer strikeouts and more homers than you'd like offset by an elite walk rate. DRA's overall reaction is summed up by that GIF of Robert Redford as Jeremiah Johnson, nodding his understated approval. Then Manaea had shoulder surgery in September that is expected to keep him out for all of 2019. A's fans' overall reaction is summed up by that GIF of Tobias Funke sobbing in the shower. It isn't so much that Manaea is Justin Verlander as that relative to the rest of the A's starting pitching the last few years, Manaea is ... well, Justin Verlander. See you in 2020, big fella.

YEAR	TEAM	LVL	AGE	WHIP	ERA	DRA	WARP	MPH	FB%	WHF	CSP
2016	NAS	AAA	24	1.11	1.50	3.12	0.5				
2016	OAK	MLB	24	1.19	3.86	4.17	2.0	95.2	58.2	12.8	47.3
2017	OAK	MLB	25	1.40	4.37	5.17	0.7	93.7	58.3	12.1	46
2018	OAK	MLB	26	1.08	3.59	4.04	2.4	92.5	56.2	10.2	53.4
2019	OAK	MLB	27	1.28	4.19	4.76	0.1	93.1	58.1	11.6	50

Sean Manaea, continued

Pitch Shape vs LHH

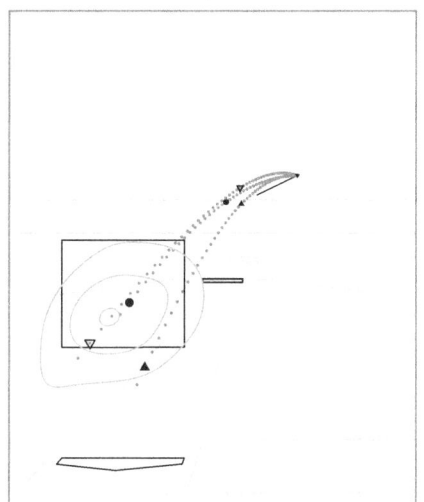

Pitch Shape vs RHH

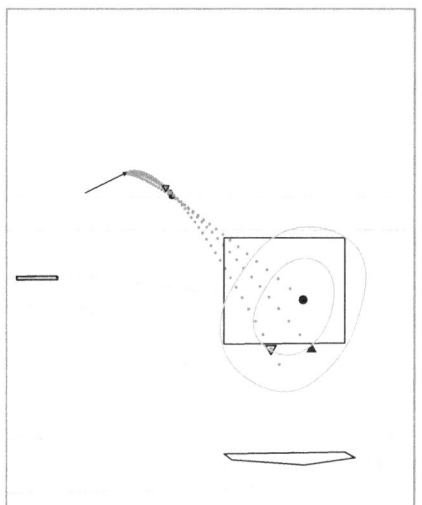

Type	Frequency	Velocity	H Movement	V Movement
● Fastball	56.2%	91.2 [96]	13.4 [69]	-20.7 [84]
□ Sinker				
+ Cutter				
▲ Changeup	31.3%	83.1 [91]	8.9 [112]	-35.1 [77]
× Splitter				
▽ Slider	12.5%	78.8 [75]	-0.8 [82]	-40.3 [78]
◇ Curveball				
⦿ Slow Curveball				
✳ Knuckleball				
▼ Screwball				

Daniel Mengden RHP

Born: 02/19/93 Age: 26 Bats: R Throws: R
Height: 6'2" Weight: 190 Origin: Round 4, 2014 Draft (#106 overall)

YEAR	TEAM	LVL	AGE	W	L	SV	G	GS	IP	H	HR	BB/9	K/9	K	GB%	BABIP
2016	MID	AA	23	2	0	0	4	4	23	15	0	4.7	11.0	28	51%	.283
2016	NAS	AAA	23	8	2	0	13	13	75^1	54	4	2.0	8.0	67	50%	.246
2016	OAK	MLB	23	2	9	0	14	14	72	83	9	4.1	8.9	71	42%	.344
2017	NAS	AAA	24	2	4	0	9	9	41	40	5	4.0	8.8	40	43%	.307
2017	OAK	MLB	24	3	2	0	7	7	43	36	6	1.9	6.1	29	40%	.240
2018	NAS	AAA	25	4	1	0	9	8	45^1	39	2	1.4	6.8	34	44%	.272
2018	OAK	MLB	25	7	6	0	22	17	115^2	103	18	2.0	5.6	72	40%	.238
2019	OAK	MLB	26	6	6	0	18	18	95	96	15	2.9	6.9	73	42%	.284

Breakout: 27% Improve: 60% Collapse: 15% Attrition: 12% MLB: 86%
Comparables: Jose Urena, Brett Oberholtzer, Erasmo Ramirez

Mengden entered last year in a battle for a back-end rotation spot, but found himself a starter by attrition after the A's injury troubles kicked off in camp. Then, through May, he posted a 2.91 ERA, and even managed a shutout. (Only 11 pitchers pitched a shutout in the AL last year.) A disastrous June led to an option to Triple-A after rehab from a foot injury rather than a return to the rotation. Mengden complicated the narrative with a 2.52 ERA in 25 innings over six games after his return to the majors in late August, pitching multiple times behind "opener" Liam Hendriks. Where does this leave him? June could have been an aberration, maybe even the result of a low-grade foot problem Mengden didn't tell anyone about until it blew up into a full-on sprain (though there's no *evidence* of this). You could therefore squint your way into seeing Mengden as a big-league starter who figured out how to be successful without impressive stuff, missing bats, getting ground balls or avoiding hard contact. Or you can avoid crow's feet, open your eyes wide, remember that the A's had the best defense in the league and regard his results with skepticism. The mustache is still aces, though.

YEAR	TEAM	LVL	AGE	WHIP	ERA	DRA	WARP	MPH	FB%	WHF	CSP
2016	MID	AA	23	1.17	0.78	3.65	0.4				
2016	NAS	AAA	23	0.94	1.67	3.33	1.7				
2016	OAK	MLB	23	1.61	6.50	5.67	-0.3	95.5	55.7	9.9	49.5
2017	NAS	AAA	24	1.41	4.17	3.49	1.0				
2017	OAK	MLB	24	1.05	3.14	4.82	0.4	94.0	56	9.3	47.6
2018	NAS	AAA	25	1.01	2.98	3.72	0.9				
2018	OAK	MLB	25	1.12	4.05	5.41	-0.2	94.2	53	8.7	51.6
2019	OAK	MLB	26	1.30	4.66	5.27	0.2	94.1	55.2	9.3	50.6

Daniel Mengden, continued

Pitch Shape vs LHH

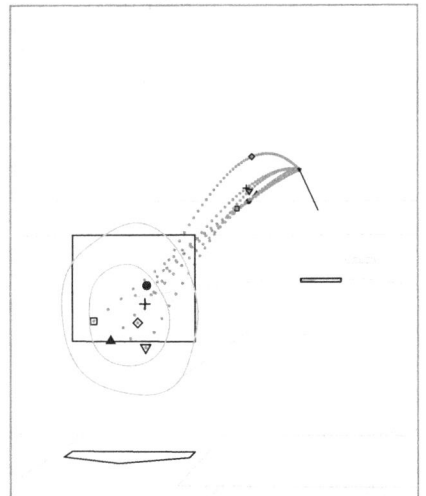

Pitch Shape vs RHH

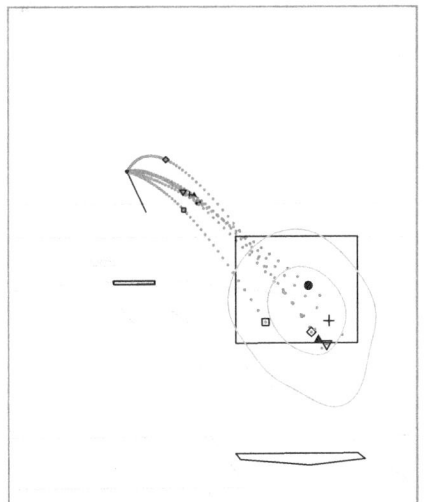

Type	Frequency	Velocity	H Movement	V Movement
● Fastball	36.9%	93.2 [102]	-5.1 [107]	-12.1 [112]
□ Sinker	16.1%	92.5 [100]	-9.6 [125]	-14.5 [119]
+ Cutter	5.0%	87.5 [92]	4.2 [113]	-28.2 [82]
▲ Changeup	13.0%	82.9 [90]	-13.2 [90]	-28.6 [96]
× Splitter				
▽ Slider	18.8%	84 [98]	5.3 [102]	-35.7 [92]
◇ Curveball	10.3%	73.2 [80]	9.3 [106]	-63.1 [66]
⊕ Slow Curveball				
✳ Knuckleball				
▼ Screwball				

Frankie Montas RHP

Born: 03/21/93 Age: 26 Bats: R Throws: R
Height: 6'2" Weight: 255 Origin: International Free Agent, 2009

YEAR	TEAM	LVL	AGE	W	L	SV	G	GS	IP	H	HR	BB/9	K/9	K	GB%	BABIP
2016	OKL	AAA	23	0	0	0	4	3	11^1	12	0	1.6	11.9	15	63%	.400
2017	OAK	MLB	24	1	1	0	23	0	32	39	10	5.6	10.1	36	36%	.349
2017	NAS	AAA	24	0	2	0	9	8	29^1	25	4	2.1	11.4	37	53%	.296
2018	NAS	AAA	25	4	5	0	15	15	71^2	69	7	3.3	7.7	61	48%	.300
2018	OAK	MLB	25	5	4	0	13	11	65	74	5	2.9	6.0	43	44%	.325
2019	OAK	MLB	26	4	5	0	29	11	74	71	10	3.3	8.0	65	46%	.291

Breakout: 30% Improve: 52% Collapse: 18% Attrition: 27% MLB: 80%
Comparables: Trevor Williams, Sergio Mitre, Tyler Duffey

The A's picked up Montas in the Rich Hill/Josh Reddick trade with the Dodgers in 2016. Hill was 36; Montas was 23. It would have been fair to assume that by 2018, Montas would be out-pitching his counterpart. It would also have been dead wrong. Montas has transitioned from a triple-digit four-seamer to a 95 mph sinker in his quest for major-league results, and he did keep the ball down last year, but he lost so many whiffs that the end product wasn't meaningfully better than he'd shown out of the bullpen in 2017. We said he was out of options last year, and that also turned out dead wrong (because his injury-marred 2016 meant he had four option seasons rather than the usual three), but this year, we swear, he's really out of options. If Montas doesn't find a way to consolidate 2018's walks with 2017's whiffs, he could spend more time on waivers than on rosters this season.

YEAR	TEAM	LVL	AGE	WHIP	ERA	DRA	WARP	MPH	FB%	WHF	CSP
2016	OKL	AAA	23	1.24	2.38	2.55	0.4				
2017	OAK	MLB	24	1.84	7.03	6.69	-0.5	100.1	66.3	12.3	49.9
2017	NAS	AAA	24	1.09	5.22	2.84	0.9				
2018	NAS	AAA	25	1.33	4.65	4.01	1.2				
2018	OAK	MLB	25	1.46	3.88	5.59	-0.2	97.6	72.5	9.4	51.3
2019	OAK	MLB	26	1.34	4.44	4.96	0.3	97.9	71.7	10.5	51.6

Frankie Montas, continued

Pitch Shape vs LHH

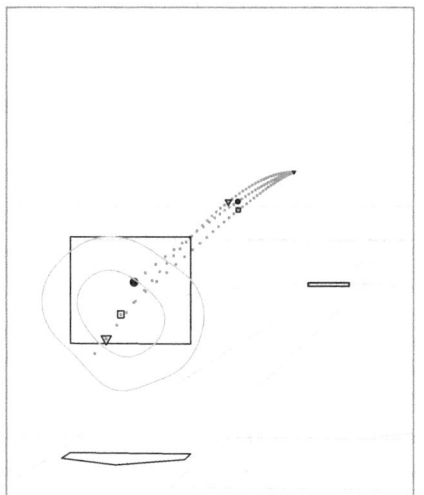

Pitch Shape vs RHH

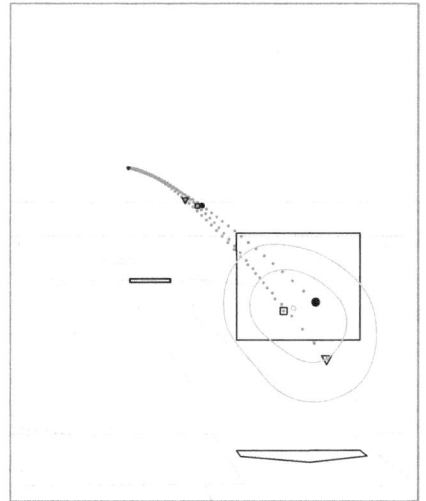

Type	Frequency	Velocity	H Movement	V Movement
● Fastball	17.5%	96.8 [114]	-4.5 [110]	-13.3 [108]
☐ Sinker	54.9%	96.1 [118]	-12.2 [103]	-17.7 [109]
+ Cutter				
▲ Changeup	2.9%	88 [111]	-13.3 [89]	-24.1 [110]
✕ Splitter				
▽ Slider	24.6%	86.5 [109]	4.6 [99]	-29.1 [111]
◇ Curveball				
✦ Slow Curveball				
✱ Knuckleball				
▼ Screwball				

Yusmeiro Petit RHP
Born: 11/22/84 Age: 34 Bats: R Throws: R
Height: 6'1" Weight: 255 Origin: International Free Agent, 2001

YEAR	TEAM	LVL	AGE	W	L	SV	G	GS	IP	H	HR	BB/9	K/9	K	GB%	BABIP
2016	WAS	MLB	31	3	5	1	36	1	62	67	12	2.2	7.1	49	44%	.291
2017	ANA	MLB	32	5	2	4	60	1	91^1	69	9	1.8	10.0	101	34%	.267
2018	OAK	MLB	33	7	3	0	74	0	93	76	13	1.7	7.4	76	36%	.241
2019	OAK	MLB	34	3	3	0	66	0	69^2	66	11	2.8	7.5	58	39%	.276

Breakout: 24% Improve: 41% Collapse: 28% Attrition: 10% MLB: 88%
Comparables: Roy Face, Rollie Fingers, Rick Aguilera

Petit, whose name belies his distinctly undainty build, parlayed a wildly successful 2017 in Anaheim into a two-year contract (with a team option) with Oakland. He took a step back last year but held onto enough of his performance that the A's may have already gotten their money's worth in a crude dollars-per-win sense. Petit remains the same soft-tossing, zone-pounding righty we've been writing about in these pages for over a decade, but as he enters his mid-30s, he's actually throwing slightly *harder* than he did when the first pitch-tracking systems came online in 2007. His curveball remains a weapon, deployed largely against righties and resulting in whiffs and weak contact, and his changeup, which he now uses almost as often as his fastball against lefties, keep hitters off balance enough to allow Petit to gobble the middle innings of close games; just under half his appearances over the last two years have gone past one inning. His stuff leaves him living on a razor's edge, but after five years of effective work, it's hard to imagine him falling off a cliff. Famous last words.

YEAR	TEAM	LVL	AGE	WHIP	ERA	DRA	WARP	MPH	FB%	WHF	CSP
2016	WAS	MLB	31	1.32	4.50	4.28	0.5	90.9	49.5	9.7	50.7
2017	ANA	MLB	32	0.95	2.76	2.83	2.4	91.2	47.8	11.6	48.5
2018	OAK	MLB	33	1.01	3.00	3.74	1.3	90.8	47.5	10	51.1
2019	OAK	MLB	34	1.25	4.74	5.07	0.1	89.9	47.3	10.4	49.4

Yusmeiro Petit, continued

Pitch Shape vs LHH

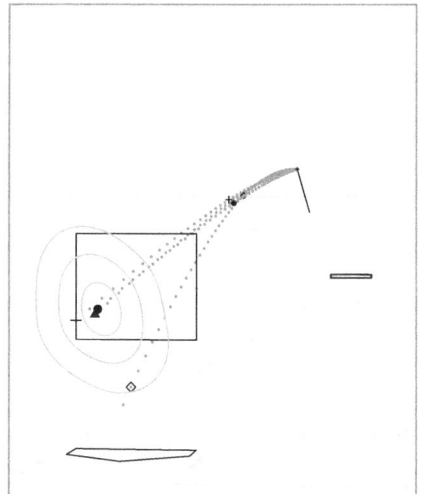

Pitch Shape vs RHH

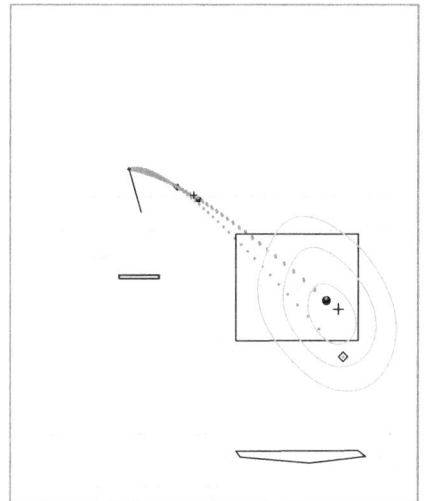

Type		Frequency	Velocity	H Movement	V Movement
●	Fastball	46.9%	90 [92]	-4.6 [109]	-14.7 [103]
□	Sinker	0.6%	89.3 [84]	-11.8 [106]	-18.8 [105]
+	Cutter	18.8%	86.1 [84]	0.2 [90]	-18.9 [119]
▲	Changeup	18.8%	82.6 [89]	-7.8 [119]	-21.6 [117]
×	Splitter				
▽	Slider				
◇	Curveball	14.8%	77.3 [96]	10.7 [112]	-37.6 [123]
⊕	Slow Curveball				
✻	Knuckleball				
▼	Screwball				

Athletics Player Analysis - 69

Fernando Rodney   RHP

Born: 03/18/77   Age: 42   Bats: R   Throws: R
Height: 5'11"   Weight: 230   Origin: International Free Agent, 1997

YEAR	TEAM	LVL	AGE	W	L	SV	G	GS	IP	H	HR	BB/9	K/9	K	GB%	BABIP
2016	SDN	MLB	39	0	1	17	28	0	28²	13	0	3.8	10.4	33	60%	.210
2016	MIA	MLB	39	2	3	8	39	0	36²	41	5	6.1	10.1	41	54%	.360
2017	ARI	MLB	40	5	4	39	61	0	55¹	40	3	4.2	10.6	65	54%	.274
2018	MIN	MLB	41	3	2	25	46	0	43²	42	5	3.9	10.3	50	45%	.319
2018	OAK	MLB	41	1	1	0	22	0	20²	20	2	5.7	8.7	20	46%	.316
2019	OAK	MLB	42	3	3	5	54	0	57	51	6	4.5	9.2	59	48%	.294

Breakout: 11%   Improve: 25%   Collapse: 23%   Attrition: 13%   MLB: 65%
Comparables: Darren Oliver, Arthur Rhodes, Roberto Hernandez

Rodney joined the A's Bullpen of Death in a mid-year trade for Low-A pitcher Dakota Chalmers and pitched well for two weeks before forgetting that the rules delimit a strike zone and permit the batter to decline to swing if the ball is not thrown in it; 13 walks in 14 2/3 innings from August 24 to the end of the year were the result. (He then added insult to insult with a disastrously brief appearance in the A's Wild Card game loss to the Yankees.) Oakland picked up his 2019 option at $5.25 million anyway, likely figuring that even in some of Rodney's good years (e.g. 2013 with Tampa Bay, 2017 with Arizona), he wasn't exactly Dennis Eckersley with the control. The much more alarming sign is the sharp fall-off in ground-ball rate. The pitch-tracking stats say that neither his sinker nor his changeup drop the way they used to; the difference, maybe an inch and a half for each, is surely imperceptible to the eye, but when the bat is only two and a half inches in diameter, an inch here and there can make a world of difference. Rodney's 42, old enough to make it extremely unlikely that he's going to get back anything he's lost.

YEAR	TEAM	LVL	AGE	WHIP	ERA	DRA	WARP	MPH	FB%	WHF	CSP
2016	SDN	MLB	39	0.87	0.31	4.21	0.3	97.3	58.4	14.7	45.6
2016	MIA	MLB	39	1.80	5.89	5.41	-0.2	97.6	57.1	12.6	41.9
2017	ARI	MLB	40	1.19	4.23	3.63	1.0	96.7	59.5	13.2	45.4
2018	MIN	MLB	41	1.40	3.09	3.85	0.5	97.0	71.8	13.1	46.8
2018	OAK	MLB	41	1.60	3.92	4.52	0.1	96.6	68.7	9.5	43.9
2019	OAK	MLB	42	1.40	4.00	4.46	0.5	95.0	61.5	12.1	43.3

Fernando Rodney, continued

Pitch Shape vs LHH

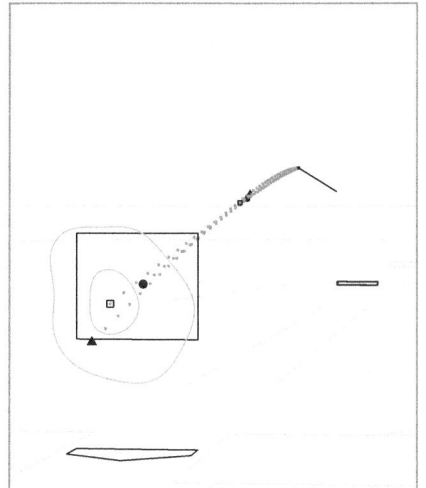

Pitch Shape vs RHH

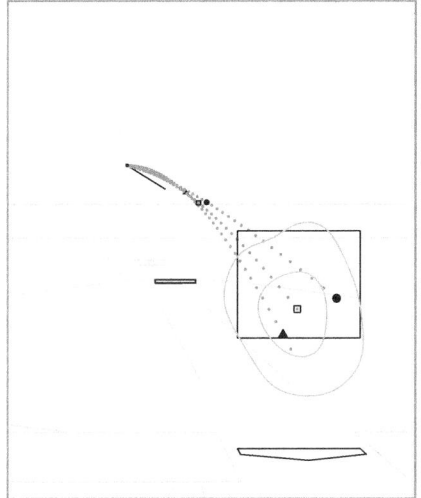

Type	Frequency	Velocity	H Movement	V Movement
● Fastball	19.8%	95.2 [109]	-4.7 [109]	-11.5 [114]
☐ Sinker	50.9%	94.2 [109]	-11 [113]	-15.9 [114]
+ Cutter				
▲ Changeup	28.8%	83.3 [92]	-12.7 [92]	-28.4 [97]
✕ Splitter				
▽ Slider	0.4%	85.3 [104]	3.4 [93]	-29.6 [110]
◇ Curveball				
✦ Slow Curveball				
✳ Knuckleball				
▼ Screwball				

Athletics Player Analysis - 71

Joakim Soria RHP

Born: 05/18/84 Age: 35 Bats: R Throws: R
Height: 6'3" Weight: 200 Origin: International Free Agent, 2001

YEAR	TEAM	LVL	AGE	W	L	SV	G	GS	IP	H	HR	BB/9	K/9	K	GB%	BABIP
2016	KCA	MLB	32	5	8	1	70	0	66²	70	10	3.6	9.2	68	52%	.323
2017	KCA	MLB	33	4	3	1	59	0	56	49	1	3.2	10.3	64	58%	.329
2018	CHA	MLB	34	0	3	16	40	0	38²	35	2	2.3	11.4	49	35%	.324
2018	MIL	MLB	34	3	1	0	26	0	22	18	2	2.5	10.6	26	48%	.286
2019	OAK	MLB	35	3	3	4	60	0	63¹	56	7	3.3	9.6	67	46%	.293

Breakout: 21% Improve: 39% Collapse: 28% Attrition: 18% MLB: 93%
Comparables: Jim Brewer, George Sherrill, Heath Bell

The era of the nameless, faceless elite reliever results from clear motivation of MLB teams: as the price of relief pitching increases, it's beneficial to take chances on some of those mid-90s fastballs or flawed two-pitch profiles reserved under minimum contracts. This ideal also leans on the thought that relievers are volatile, and there are very few who'll repeat elite, high-leverage performances on an annual basis. Soria straddled both edges of this thinking in 2018, recovering his status as an excellent closer after converting just two saves in 2016-2017, while also reinventing himself in a manner that almost makes him unrecognizable to the classic Soria of yore. The former changeup savant dropped his release point and embraced a slider, giving a new look to batters and producing his best results in years. A slider-heavy Soria may be nameless, faceless after all, for he's now swimming in uncharted waters as a wily, inventive veteran.

YEAR	TEAM	LVL	AGE	WHIP	ERA	DRA	WARP	MPH	FB%	WHF	CSP
2016	KCA	MLB	32	1.46	4.05	3.47	1.1	95.2	62.2	12.5	48.6
2017	KCA	MLB	33	1.23	3.70	3.62	1.0	94.7	49.3	13.5	46.6
2018	CHA	MLB	34	1.16	2.56	2.35	1.1	94.2	63	15.4	45.8
2018	MIL	MLB	34	1.09	4.09	2.94	0.5	94.4	71.2	14.2	50.1
2019	OAK	MLB	35	1.25	3.57	4.11	0.8	93.4	58.6	13.6	46.6

Joakim Soria, continued

Pitch Shape vs LHH

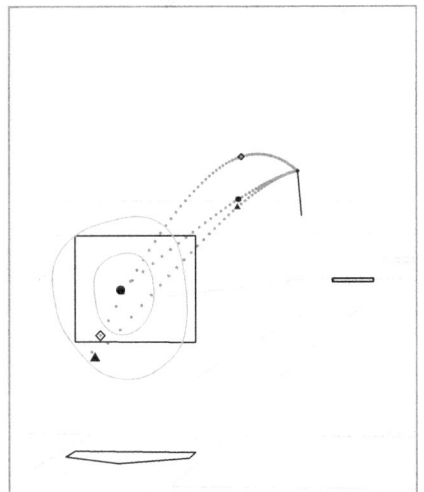

Pitch Shape vs RHH

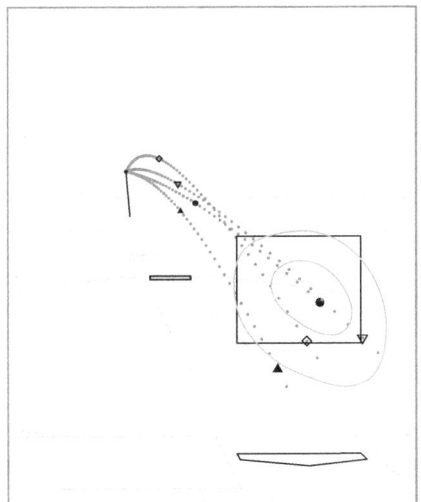

Type	Frequency	Velocity	H Movement	V Movement
● Fastball	65.3%	92.9 [101]	-3 [117]	-14.1 [105]
□ Sinker	0.7%	91.7 [96]	-12.3 [102]	-24.8 [85]
+ Cutter				
▲ Changeup	15.1%	87.4 [108]	-6.5 [125]	-27.4 [100]
× Splitter				
▽ Slider	10.9%	79 [76]	16.3 [149]	-40.2 [79]
◇ Curveball	8.1%	70.9 [72]	11.7 [116]	-66.4 [59]
⊕ Slow Curveball				
✳ Knuckleball				
▼ Screwball				

Blake Treinen RHP
Born: 06/30/88 Age: 31 Bats: R Throws: R
Height: 6'5" Weight: 225 Origin: Round 7, 2011 Draft (#226 overall)

YEAR	TEAM	LVL	AGE	W	L	SV	G	GS	IP	H	HR	BB/9	K/9	K	GB%	BABIP
2016	WAS	MLB	28	4	1	1	73	0	67	51	5	4.2	8.5	63	67%	.280
2017	WAS	MLB	29	0	2	3	37	0	37²	48	3	3.1	7.6	32	62%	.381
2017	OAK	MLB	29	3	4	13	35	0	38	32	3	2.8	9.9	42	60%	.299
2018	OAK	MLB	30	9	2	38	68	0	80¹	46	2	2.4	11.2	100	53%	.232
2019	OAK	MLB	31	3	3	36	60	0	63¹	49	5	3.6	10.4	73	55%	.290

Breakout: 17% Improve: 36% Collapse: 30% Attrition: 10% MLB: 90%
Comparables: Tony Watson, Francisco Cordero, Mark Melancon

Treinen, who still has two more years of team control before free agency, built on his excellent half-season in the A's closer role in 2017 with the kind of performance that might have won him a Cy Young award in less enlightened times. As it is, he finished sixth in the AL voting, powered by the fifth-best reliever ERA (min. 50 IP) since 1946. He gets the job done largely with an unbarrelable, nigh untouchable 96–99 mph sinker; the only pitcher in baseball with a similar combination of whiffs and grounders on a high-usage sinker is Zach Britton. Treinen didn't reach pro ball until he was 23, and the majors at 26, so while it seems like he's just arrived, he's only a month younger than, to pick a name out of a hat, Craig Kimbrel. Odds are, then, that 2018 was a peak, not a plateau, but Edmund Hillary didn't make his home atop Everest and you know who he is anyway, so what's the difference in the long run?

YEAR	TEAM	LVL	AGE	WHIP	ERA	DRA	WARP	MPH	FB%	WHF	CSP
2016	WAS	MLB	28	1.22	2.28	4.59	0.3	98.1	68.7	11.6	47.1
2017	WAS	MLB	29	1.62	5.73	4.79	0.2	99.0	72.6	13.1	46.9
2017	OAK	MLB	29	1.16	2.13	3.96	0.5	98.9	61.8	14.3	48.3
2018	OAK	MLB	30	0.83	0.78	2.22	2.5	99.1	67.1	19.2	47.7
2019	OAK	MLB	31	1.17	2.78	3.39	1.3	97.9	67.1	15.5	47.2

Blake Treinen, continued

Pitch Shape vs LHH

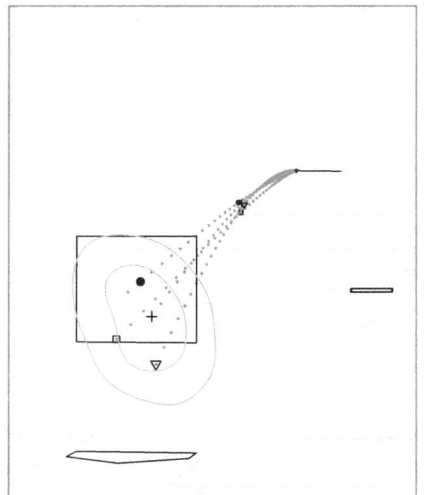

Pitch Shape vs RHH

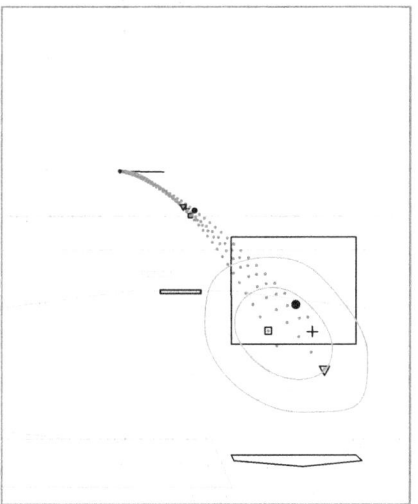

Type		Frequency	Velocity	H Movement	V Movement
●	Fastball	18.4%	98.2 [118]	-5.8 [104]	-14.2 [105]
□	Sinker	48.7%	98 [127]	-13.7 [91]	-21.9 [95]
+	Cutter	11.5%	94.3 [133]	2.4 [103]	-21.6 [109]
▲	Changeup				
×	Splitter				
▽	Slider	21.4%	89.7 [123]	4.8 [100]	-34 [97]
◇	Curveball				
✦	Slow Curveball				
✸	Knuckleball				
▼	Screwball				

Oakland Athletics 2019

Andrew Triggs RHP
Born: 03/16/89 Age: 30 Bats: R Throws: R
Height: 6'4" Weight: 220 Origin: Round 19, 2012 Draft (#583 overall)

YEAR	TEAM	LVL	AGE	W	L	SV	G	GS	IP	H	HR	BB/9	K/9	K	GB%	BABIP
2016	NAS	AAA	27	2	1	2	16	0	18^1	16	0	2.5	10.3	21	59%	.314
2016	OAK	MLB	27	1	1	0	24	6	56^1	56	5	2.1	8.8	55	52%	.315
2017	OAK	MLB	28	5	6	0	12	12	65^1	68	9	2.6	6.9	50	49%	.294
2018	OAK	MLB	29	3	1	0	9	9	41^1	37	7	3.9	9.4	43	49%	.270
2019	OAK	MLB	30	2	1	0	30	0	31^2	27	3	3.4	8.6	30	48%	.287

Breakout: 20% Improve: 41% Collapse: 23% Attrition: 20% MLB: 75%
Comparables: Kevin Gregg, Phil Coke, Alex Wilson

Keeping Triggs healthy has proven harder than remembering whether it's the cosecant or the secant that's the inverse of the sine. Last year's injury was nerve irritation in his pitching arm, which kept him out after mid-May (aside from a single rehab appearance in Stockton in September) and resulted in surgery to relieve thoracic outlet syndrome in late September. His outlook for 2019, or indeed his career, is unknown as this book goes to press. If Triggs does get back on the mound, he'll resume his attempt at a fifth-starter career, or maybe find himself as a useful multi-inning pitcher on one of these "no starters" pitching staffs we seem to be barreling toward.

YEAR	TEAM	LVL	AGE	WHIP	ERA	DRA	WARP	MPH	FB%	WHF	CSP
2016	NAS	AAA	27	1.15	2.95	2.19	0.6				
2016	OAK	MLB	27	1.22	4.31	3.63	1.0	92.8	55.4	10.7	48.1
2017	OAK	MLB	28	1.33	4.27	4.53	0.8	91.1	43.9	10.6	46.8
2018	OAK	MLB	29	1.33	5.23	5.57	-0.1	91.2	48.5	10.6	45.1
2019	OAK	MLB	30	1.23	3.50	4.05	0.4	90.9	48.3	10.6	46.3

Andrew Triggs, continued

Pitch Shape vs LHH

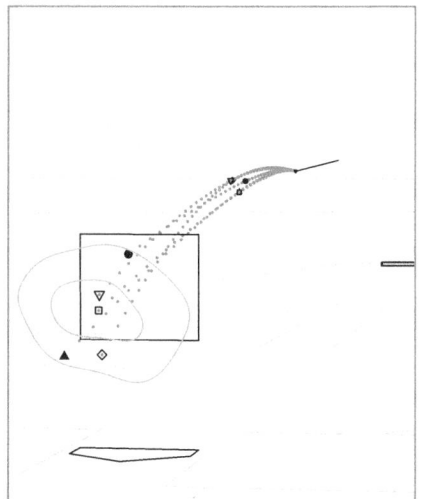

Pitch Shape vs RHH

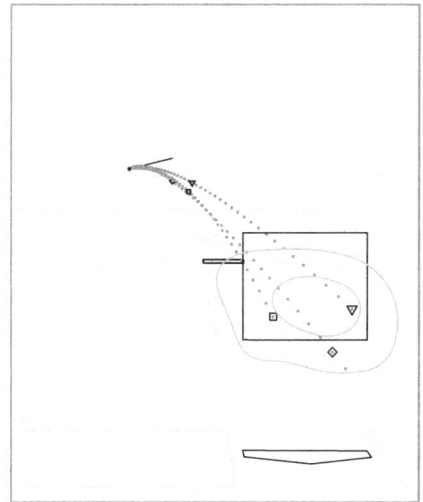

Type	Frequency	Velocity	H Movement	V Movement
● Fastball	6.5%	89.9 [92]	-7.6 [96]	-20.4 [85]
☐ Sinker	42.0%	90.2 [89]	-12.8 [99]	-29.3 [71]
+ Cutter				
▲ Changeup	7.5%	83.6 [93]	-12.6 [93]	-36.8 [72]
✕ Splitter				
▽ Slider	21.0%	84.2 [99]	4.7 [99]	-32.1 [103]
◇ Curveball	22.9%	76.7 [93]	14.8 [129]	-45.3 [106]
⊕ Slow Curveball				
✳ Knuckleball				
▼ Screwball				

Lou Trivino RHP

Born: 10/01/91   Age: 27   Bats: R   Throws: R
Height: 6'5"   Weight: 225   Origin: Round 11, 2013 Draft (#341 overall)

YEAR	TEAM	LVL	AGE	W	L	SV	G	GS	IP	H	HR	BB/9	K/9	K	GB%	BABIP
2016	STO	A+	24	1	3	2	33	0	41^2	38	0	3.9	10.6	49	61%	.342
2016	MID	AA	24	1	1	1	12	0	18^1	14	1	3.4	5.9	12	48%	.236
2017	MID	AA	25	7	1	1	23	0	33^1	31	0	2.7	9.2	34	57%	.333
2017	NAS	AAA	25	1	2	4	25	0	35	33	0	2.8	8.0	31	54%	.308
2018	OAK	MLB	26	8	3	4	69	1	74	53	8	3.8	10.0	82	47%	.256
2019	OAK	MLB	27	3	3	2	60	0	63^1	52	6	4.2	9.8	69	48%	.289

Breakout: 15%   Improve: 34%   Collapse: 22%   Attrition: 20%   MLB: 68%
Comparables: Michael Blazek, Tom Mastny, Zach Putnam

Any decent Hell Bullpen needs one guy like Trivino to leap out of the minors with no prospect pedigree and throw untouchable smoke while steadily earning a more central role than could have been anticipated in spring training. Trivino brings heat at 97 mph about half the time, split between a sinking and a straight fastball. His main secondary pitch is classified as a cutter, and comes in at 92, but in the context of his other fastballs, it comes across more like a very tight slider. His whiff rate on the pitch is elite, in the top 10 percent of the league, and of the pitchers in his vicinity, only Alex Colome throws his as often as Trivino does. The resulting three-fastballs, no-secondaries, lots-of-strikeouts approach is not *unique* (check out Ryan Tepera, for instance, or Dominic Leone), but it's still unusual and should make Trivino one of the more intriguing setup men in the league.

YEAR	TEAM	LVL	AGE	WHIP	ERA	DRA	WARP	MPH	FB%	WHF	CSP
2016	STO	A+	24	1.34	3.02	3.46	0.8				
2016	MID	AA	24	1.15	2.45	3.09	0.4				
2017	MID	AA	25	1.23	2.43	3.34	0.6				
2017	NAS	AAA	25	1.26	3.60	2.94	0.9				
2018	OAK	MLB	26	1.14	2.92	3.10	1.6	98.9	53.7	15.1	47.8
2019	OAK	MLB	27	1.29	3.51	4.05	0.8	98.4	54.3	15.3	48.4

Lou Trivino, continued

Pitch Shape vs LHH

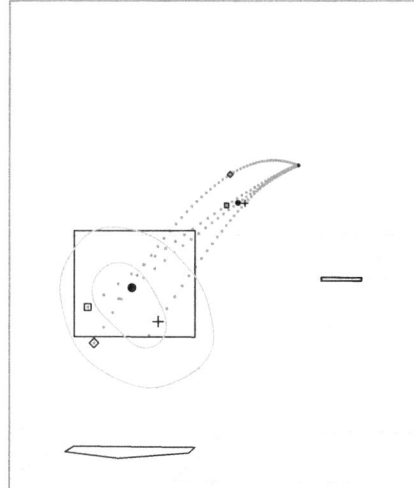

Pitch Shape vs RHH

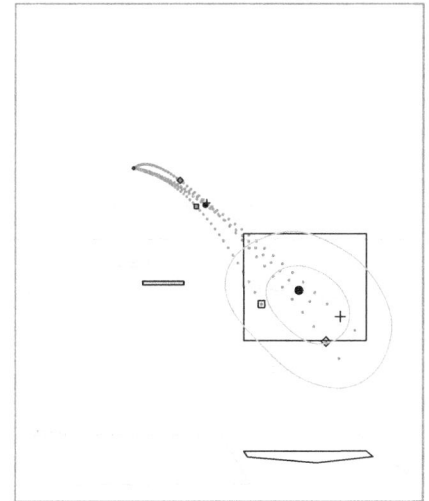

Type	Frequency	Velocity	H Movement	V Movement
● Fastball	34.2%	98.2 [118]	-6.9 [99]	-12.7 [110]
□ Sinker	19.5%	98.4 [130]	-13.6 [92]	-17.4 [110]
+ Cutter	38.8%	93 [125]	3.3 [109]	-21.8 [108]
▲ Changeup	1.0%	88.9 [114]	-13.4 [89]	-28.5 [97]
× Splitter				
▽ Slider				
◇ Curveball	6.6%	81.7 [112]	12.5 [119]	-46.1 [104]
⊕ Slow Curveball				
✳ Knuckleball				
▼ Screwball				

Lazaro Armenteros LF

Born: 05/22/99 Age: 20 Bats: R Throws: R
Height: 6'0" Weight: 182 Origin: International Free Agent, 2016

YEAR	TEAM	LVL	AGE	PA	R	2B	3B	HR	RBI	BB	K	SB	CS	AVG/OBP/SLG
2017	DAT	RK	18	26	6	0	0	0	1	3	9	2	2	.167/.385/.167
2017	ATH	RK	18	181	24	9	4	4	22	16	48	10	1	.288/.376/.474
2018	BLT	A	19	340	43	8	2	8	39	36	115	8	6	.277/.374/.401
2019	OAK	MLB	20	251	24	5	0	7	22	11	102	1	1	.168/.211/.279

Breakout: 4% Improve: 4% Collapse: 0% Attrition: 2% MLB: 4%
Comparables: Clint Frazier, Caleb Gindl, Chris Parmelee

Armenteros was one of just 11 teenage hitters in the Midwest League, yet he led his team in on-base percentage, a testament to the fact that he's a *hitter*, not merely a tools monster. Of course, he has tools, too: Analysts continue to talk up his future power, premised on excellent bat speed, but it hasn't shown up in games yet; it will need to, because he's already a left fielder, and is not likely to move back to center as he advances up the ladder. Armenteros missed a month of the season after appearing to injure his knee beating out an infield single. He departed with a .454 slugging percentage, and finished the year just a hair over .400. Correlation isn't causation, but considering how little information comes out of the minor leagues on injuries, one might wonder whether his base was fully stable under him (or whether he trusted it) after he came back.

YEAR	TEAM	LVL	AGE	PA	DRC+	VORP	BABIP	BRR	FRAA	WARP
2017	DAT	RK	18	26	37	2.0	.300	0.9	CF(6): 1.5	0.2
2017	ATH	RK	18	181	112	14.2	.387	2.8	LF(28): 4.2, CF(2): -0.5	0.4
2018	BLT	A	19	340	119	21.6	.427	2.1	LF(69): -0.7	1.1
2019	OAK	MLB	20	251	29	-14.8	.255	-0.4	LF 2	-1.4

Austin Beck CF

Born: 11/21/98 Age: 20 Bats: R Throws: R
Height: 6'1" Weight: 200 Origin: Round 1, 2017 Draft (#6 overall)

YEAR	TEAM	LVL	AGE	PA	R	2B	3B	HR	RBI	BB	K	SB	CS	AVG/OBP/SLG
2017	ATH	RK	18	174	23	7	4	2	28	17	51	7	1	.211/.293/.349
2018	BLT	A	19	534	58	29	4	2	60	30	117	8	6	.296/.335/.383
2019	OAK	MLB	20	251	15	5	0	5	21	4	83	0	0	.159/.171/.242

Breakout: 1%   Improve: 1%   Collapse: 0%   Attrition: 0%   MLB: 1%
Comparables: Engel Beltre, Carlos Tocci, Gorkys Hernandez

Beck came into pro ball in 2017 with all the tools in the world and no idea what to do with them. In 2018, as one of the youngest hitters in the Midwest League (along with teammate Lazaro Armenteros), he started figuring out one piece: putting the wood bat on the pitched baseball. Over-the-fence power is the next hurdle, and there's every physical indication he'll clear it, though if he moves to the Cal League this year as expected, it may be tough to sort out the genuine improvement from the environmental help. He's still nowhere near the majors, and plenty of youngsters never translate strength into game pop, but Beck has at least checked the first box: not being overmatched by full-season ball.

YEAR	TEAM	LVL	AGE	PA	DRC+	VORP	BABIP	BRR	FRAA	WARP
2017	ATH	RK	18	174	50	2.6	.294	1.8	CF(33): 1.2	-0.5
2018	BLT	A	19	534	105	14.9	.377	-4.8	CF(113): 2.0	0.9
2019	OAK	MLB	20	251	1	-20.6	.214	-0.3	CF -1	-2.4

Jorge Mateo SS
Born: 06/23/95 Age: 24 Bats: R Throws: R
Height: 6'0" Weight: 190 Origin: International Free Agent, 2012

YEAR	TEAM	LVL	AGE	PA	R	2B	3B	HR	RBI	BB	K	SB	CS	AVG/OBP/SLG
2016	TAM	A+	21	507	65	16	9	8	47	33	108	36	15	.254/.306/.379
2017	TAM	A+	22	297	39	16	8	4	11	16	79	28	3	.240/.288/.400
2017	TRN	AA	22	140	26	9	3	4	26	15	32	11	7	.300/.381/.525
2017	MID	AA	22	147	25	5	7	4	20	9	33	13	3	.292/.333/.518
2018	NAS	AAA	23	510	50	17	16	3	45	29	139	25	10	.230/.280/.353
2019	OAK	MLB	24	71	8	3	2	1	6	3	22	3	1	.212/.254/.364

Breakout: 13% Improve: 20% Collapse: 0% Attrition: 18% MLB: 23%
Comparables: Grant Green, Erik Gonzalez, Juan Diaz

Spending a full year at Triple-A in your age-23 season is good; a .633 OPS, even from a shortstop, is substantially less so. Mateo is in danger of becoming a classic "can't steal first" player, though at the efficiency level he showed last year, he might get thrown out trying to do that, too. (Twenty-five steals in 35 attempts is not actually horrible; it's just striking when someone with 80-grade speed doesn't steal at a 90-percent-plus rate.) His plate discipline suffered against the advanced pitching he faced in the PCL, and his line is a good reminder that plate discipline doesn't just mean drawing walks; it also means waiting for pitches to drive. Mateo is young enough to spend another year at Triple-A trying to figure things out, but his roster situation means there's a clock on his development: He came stateside so long ago that he's already entering his *third* season on a 40-man roster (and therefore his third option year) without approaching the majors. Having just one fewer triple than double for the season is pretty cool, though.

YEAR	TEAM	LVL	AGE	PA	DRC+	VORP	BABIP	BRR	FRAA	WARP
2016	TAM	A+	21	507	95	11.8	.313	3.2	SS(62): -5.1, 2B(40): -0.6	0.2
2017	TAM	A+	22	297	89	15.4	.321	7.6	SS(42): 2.9, CF(22): -0.8	1.1
2017	TRN	AA	22	140	124	17.0	.372	1.6	SS(17): 1.1, CF(7): -0.4	0.9
2017	MID	AA	22	147	104	14.2	.356	2.2	SS(30): 0.8	0.7
2018	NAS	AAA	23	510	58	3.7	.316	1.1	SS(123): -0.8, 2B(4): -0.5	-0.8
2019	OAK	MLB	24	71	59	-0.1	.293	0.6	SS 0	0.0

Sean Murphy C

Born: 10/10/94 Age: 24 Bats: R Throws: R
Height: 6'3" Weight: 215 Origin: Round 3, 2016 Draft (#83 overall)

YEAR	TEAM	LVL	AGE	PA	R	2B	3B	HR	RBI	BB	K	SB	CS	AVG/OBP/SLG
2016	VER	A-	21	85	10	1	0	2	7	9	12	1	0	.237/.318/.329
2017	STO	A+	22	178	22	11	0	9	26	11	33	0	0	.297/.343/.527
2017	MID	AA	22	217	25	7	0	4	22	21	34	0	0	.209/.288/.309
2018	MID	AA	23	289	51	26	2	8	43	23	47	3	0	.288/.358/.498
2019	OAK	MLB	24	65	5	2	0	2	7	3	14	0	0	.183/.222/.317

Breakout: 8% Improve: 26% Collapse: 0% Attrition: 23% MLB: 43%
Comparables: Mitch Garver, Jonathan Lucroy, Josh Donaldson

Murphy has now worked his way from undrafted walk-on to third-round pick to top-five catching prospect. The bat was suspect, but a return engagement in the Texas League saw him knock a ton of extra-base hits (though mostly

YEAR	TEAM	P. COUNT	FRM RUNS	BLK RUNS	THRW RUNS	TOT RUNS
2017	MID	7267	3.6	-0.5	0.2	2.7
2018	MID	8864	13.6	1.4	0.6	15.6
2019	OAK	2378	1.0	0.0	-0.2	0.8

inside the fences), at least until his second broken hamate in three years wiped out most of July and August. His arm remains the sexiest part of his toolkit, but we've learned in recent years that the arm is a small part of the overall catching package, and it's only gotten smaller as teams push station-to-station baseball to the outer limits of possibility. Murphy may not be a preternaturally gifted stealer of strikes with his pitch-receiving, but reports on that front are positive, and professional coaching can work wonders for players who have the athleticism and attitude to implement those lessons. His arrival in the major leagues has now become more "when" than "if." At this writing, the A's no. 1 catcher is Josh Phegley; if that doesn't change, the "when" might be answered by looking up the next Southwest flight from McCarran to Oakland.

YEAR	TEAM	LVL	AGE	PA	DRC+	VORP	BABIP	BRR	FRAA	WARP
2016	VER	A-	21	85	102	3.1	.258	0.4	C(20): 0.4	0.3
2017	STO	A+	22	178	132	15.1	.323	0.2	C(40): -0.3	0.9
2017	MID	AA	22	217	62	1.8	.232	0.6	C(51): 3.8	0.1
2018	MID	AA	23	289	133	22.6	.324	2.1	C(65): 14.5	3.4
2019	OAK	MLB	24	65	37	-2.0	.205	-0.1	C 1	-0.2

Sheldon Neuse 3B

Born: 12/10/94   Age: 24   Bats: R   Throws: R
Height: 6'0"   Weight: 195   Origin: Round 2, 2016 Draft (#58 overall)

YEAR	TEAM	LVL	AGE	PA	R	2B	3B	HR	RBI	BB	K	SB	CS	AVG/OBP/SLG
2016	AUB	A-	21	141	16	5	3	1	11	13	26	2	2	.230/.305/.341
2017	HAG	A	22	321	40	19	3	9	51	25	66	12	5	.291/.349/.469
2017	STO	A+	22	94	21	3	0	7	22	9	25	2	0	.386/.457/.675
2017	MID	AA	22	75	9	4	0	0	6	6	21	0	0	.373/.427/.433
2018	NAS	AAA	23	537	48	26	3	5	55	32	172	4	1	.263/.304/.357
2019	OAK	MLB	24	251	22	10	1	5	25	11	85	1	0	.240/.275/.351

Breakout: 3%   Improve: 9%   Collapse: 0%   Attrition: 8%   MLB: 10%
Comparables: Patrick Wisdom, Russell Mitchell, Luke Hughes

After a 2017 breakout, Neuse simply failed his Triple-A test in 2018. There's plenty of time for him to try the PCL again, and plenty of reason to think his quick ascent to the high minors was not a fluke. (He was a major-college second-round pick, after all, not some up-from-nothing $2,500-bonus surprise case.) There's no real hurry because there's no place for him to play in Oakland anyway. He's going to have to force the issue, and a .357 slugging percentage doesn't force anything except gun jokes. Speaking of which, Neuse has a pistol right arm and might try relief pitching if the batting thing doesn't work out; it would only be appropriate, seeing how he came to the A's in the Sean Doolittle trade.

YEAR	TEAM	LVL	AGE	PA	DRC+	VORP	BABIP	BRR	FRAA	WARP
2016	AUB	A-	21	141	90	3.9	.280	-0.4	3B(26): 1.9, SS(6): 1.0	0.2
2017	HAG	A	22	321	144	27.3	.347	-1.9	SS(43): -2.9, 3B(33): 6.6	2.4
2017	STO	A+	22	94	218	16.9	.490	0.4	3B(10): -1.5, SS(8): -0.4	1.1
2017	MID	AA	22	75	140	4.7	.532	0.3	3B(18): 1.4, 1B(1): -0.4	0.5
2018	NAS	AAA	23	537	75	11.4	.385	-0.4	3B(130): -3.1, SS(1): 0.7	-0.6
2019	OAK	MLB	24	251	68	-4.0	.350	-0.2	3B 1, 2B 0	-0.3

Grant Holmes RHP

Born: 03/22/96 Age: 23 Bats: L Throws: R
Height: 6'1" Weight: 215 Origin: Round 1, 2014 Draft (#22 overall)

YEAR	TEAM	LVL	AGE	W	L	SV	G	GS	IP	H	HR	BB/9	K/9	K	GB%	BABIP
2016	RCU	A+	20	8	4	1	20	18	105^1	103	6	3.7	8.5	100	53%	.316
2016	STO	A+	20	3	3	0	6	5	28^2	44	4	3.1	7.5	24	60%	.408
2017	MID	AA	21	11	12	0	29	24	148^1	149	15	3.7	9.1	150	46%	.328
2018	STO	A+	22	0	0	0	2	2	6	4	1	3.0	12.0	8	47%	.214
2019	*OAK*	*MLB*	*23*	*1*	*1*	*0*	*3*	*3*	*15*	*14*	*1*	*3.9*	*8.5*	*14*	*44%*	*.294*

Breakout: 18% Improve: 28% Collapse: 9% Attrition: 37% MLB: 48%
Comparables: Justin Wilson, Wily Peralta, Scott Barnes

Holmes pitched two High-A games in late August after missing the entire season with a rotator cuff injury; he was then shut down again and his 2019 status is unknown as of this writing. He left off 2017 with mid-rotation upside driven by intriguing command of his fastball and curve, but a strong possibility of a bullpen future due to a missing third pitch. Now, who knows. (The former first-round pick was added to the 40-man roster in November because he would have been eligible for the Rule 5 draft.) For all the criticism of the overly simplistic analysis that the term sometimes leads us toward, this is a big part of the reason Gary Huckabay started using "TINSTAAPP" in the first place.

YEAR	TEAM	LVL	AGE	WHIP	ERA	DRA	WARP	MPH	FB%	WHF	CSP
2016	RCU	A+	20	1.39	4.02	3.64	2.2				
2016	STO	A+	20	1.88	6.91	3.52	0.6				
2017	MID	AA	21	1.42	4.49	3.75	2.4				
2018	STO	A+	22	1.00	4.50	3.90	0.1				
2019	*OAK*	*MLB*	*23*	*1.37*	*4.20*	*4.77*	*0.1*				

Oakland Athletics 2019

Jesus Luzardo LHP

Born: 09/30/97   Age: 21   Bats: L   Throws: L
Height: 6'1"   Weight: 205   Origin: Round 3, 2016 Draft (#94 overall)

YEAR	TEAM	LVL	AGE	W	L	SV	G	GS	IP	H	HR	BB/9	K/9	K	GB%	BABIP
2017	NAT	RK	19	1	0	0	3	3	13²	14	1	0.0	9.9	15	33%	.342
2017	ATH	RK	19	0	1	0	4	3	11²	9	0	0.8	10.0	13	58%	.290
2017	VER	A-	19	1	0	0	5	5	18	12	1	2.0	10.0	20	53%	.250
2018	STO	A+	20	2	1	0	3	3	14²	6	0	3.1	15.3	25	56%	.240
2018	MID	AA	20	7	3	0	16	16	78²	58	5	2.1	9.8	86	46%	.268
2018	NAS	AAA	20	1	1	0	4	4	16	25	2	3.9	10.1	18	51%	.469
2019	OAK	MLB	21	7	7	0	23	23	115	103	14	2.9	9.3	119	43%	.290

Breakout: 9%   Improve: 16%   Collapse: 8%   Attrition: 17%   MLB: 30%
Comparables: Henry Owens, Drew Hutchison, Shelby Miller

Last year, we told you not to "expect to see Luzardo set loose on the Midwest League" because 2016 Tommy John surgery meant his pro experience to that point had been limited and carefully managed. We were right, in the sense that Luzardo was instead set loose on the *Texas League* en route to a brief PCL experience after dumping the Cal League straight in the trash. (He still averaged less than five innings per start, though.) He's now in the proverbial conversation for best pitching prospect in the game, which is what happens when you bring mid-90s heat from the left side, a plus changeup to combat righties, an improving curveball and, most importantly, beyond-his-years knowledge of how convert his arsenal into outs. The difficult reality of Major League Baseball is that even no. 2 and 3 starters used to be extremely good prospects, and that's probably what Luzardo is in the majors, not a no. 1. He could start reaching that ceiling as soon as this year, minus the requisite few weeks to "work on some things" (read: ensure seven years until free agency rather than six) that will surely be imposed just as they are on every prospect who should be on an Opening Day roster until something is changed to create incentives for teams to always use their best available players in the major leagues.

YEAR	TEAM	LVL	AGE	WHIP	ERA	DRA	WARP	MPH	FB%	WHF	CSP
2017	NAT	RK	19	1.02	1.32	2.01	0.6				
2017	ATH	RK	19	0.86	1.54	2.73	0.4				
2017	VER	A-	19	0.89	2.00	2.56	0.6				
2018	STO	A+	20	0.75	1.23	1.70	0.6				
2018	MID	AA	20	0.97	2.29	3.40	1.8				
2018	NAS	AAA	20	2.00	7.31	2.90	0.5				
2019	OAK	MLB	21	1.21	3.82	4.33	1.5				

A.J. Puk LHP

Born: 04/25/95 Age: 24 Bats: L Throws: L
Height: 6'7" Weight: 220 Origin: Round 1, 2016 Draft (#6 overall)

YEAR	TEAM	LVL	AGE	W	L	SV	G	GS	IP	H	HR	BB/9	K/9	K	GB%	BABIP
2016	VER	A-	21	0	4	0	10	10	32²	23	0	3.3	11.0	40	51%	.271
2017	STO	A+	22	4	5	0	14	11	61	44	1	3.4	14.5	98	42%	.336
2017	MID	AA	22	2	5	0	13	13	64	64	2	3.5	12.1	86	48%	.380
2019	*OAK*	*MLB*	*24*	*3*	*2*	*0*	*8*	*8*	*42*	*38*	*5*	*4.0*	*9.4*	*44*	*41%*	*.296*

Breakout: 13% Improve: 26% Collapse: 12% Attrition: 24% MLB: 40%
Comparables: Edwar Cabrera, Matt Barnes, Dan Meyer

Puk entered 2018 as the A's best prospect, a hard-throwing lefty with a wipeout slider and a real shot at joining the rotation after a few phantom "development" weeks in Triple-A. He ended March on the shelf and had Tommy John surgery in early April. Puk had finished 2017 still needing to show the kind of mechanical consistency that will let him attack the zone or miss it with intent rather than throwing his best stuff in the general vicinity of the catcher and seeing what happens. A healthy camp might have shown us that a winter of work had leveled him up in that area; instead, it remains a question mark. Even if he never applies those finishing touches, though, the downside may not be what it once was: Rather than a boring traditional eighth-inning guy, one could dream of a Josh Hader/Andrew Miller-style weapon.

YEAR	TEAM	LVL	AGE	WHIP	ERA	DRA	WARP	MPH	FB%	WHF	CSP
2016	VER	A-	21	1.07	3.03	2.67	1.0				
2017	STO	A+	22	1.10	3.69	2.11	2.2				
2017	MID	AA	22	1.39	4.36	2.91	1.7				
2019	*OAK*	*MLB*	*24*	*1.37*	*3.90*	*4.43*	*0.5*				

Oakland Athletics 2019

LINEOUTS

Hitters

HITTER	POS	TEAM	LVL	AGE	PA	R	2B	3B	HR	RBI	BB	K	SB	CS	AVG/OBP/SLG	DRC+	WARP
Nick Allen	SS	BLT	A	19	512	51	17	6	0	34	34	85	24	8	.239/.301/.302	76	1.1
Greg Deichmann	OF	ATH	Rk	23	43	9	2	2	1	7	5	8	0	0	.289/.372/.526	125	0.0
	OF	STO	A+	23	185	18	14	0	6	21	17	63	0	1	.199/.276/.392	66	-0.8
Jeremy Eierman	SS	VER	A-	21	267	36	8	2	8	26	13	70	10	4	.235/.283/.381	76	-0.3
Jameson Hannah	OF	VER	A-	20	95	14	4	1	1	10	9	24	6	0	.279/.347/.384	125	0.0
Chris Herrmann	RF	TAC	AAA	30	174	26	3	1	6	24	36	42	0	0	.257/.416/.426	133	0.9
	RF	SEA	MLB	30	87	6	4	2	2	7	10	24	0	0	.237/.322/.421	91	0.3
Corban Joseph	INF	BOW	AA	29	523	73	30	2	17	68	52	43	8	2	.312/.381/.497	146	2.1
	INF	BAL	MLB	29	19	1	1	0	0	3	1	5	0	0	.222/.263/.278	81	-0.1
Kevin Merrell	SS	STO	A+	22	290	38	10	3	0	24	15	66	5	4	.267/.308/.326	88	-0.3
Cliff Pennington	SS	CIN	MLB	34	34	1	0	0	0	0	5	13	0	0	.138/.265/.138	57	-0.1
	SS	LOU	AAA	34	37	4	2	0	0	1	6	7	0	1	.267/.378/.333	123	0.2
	SS	ROU	AAA	34	250	26	12	1	1	13	30	54	4	1	.204/.301/.282	64	-0.2
Josh Phegley	C	NAS	AAA	30	139	12	6	3	3	18	15	31	0	0	.235/.331/.412	102	0.6
	C	OAK	MLB	30	102	13	7	0	2	15	6	27	0	0	.204/.255/.344	75	0.1
Tyler Ramirez	OF	MID	AA	23	594	73	35	4	10	79	62	148	5	4	.287/.370/.430	113	0.7
Beau Taylor	C	NAS	AAA	28	356	39	15	3	3	39	50	89	2	0	.248/.360/.348	95	0.9
	C	OAK	MLB	28	6	0	1	0	0	0	1	2	0	0	.200/.333/.400	85	0.0

Nick Allen got the bat knocked out of his hands in Low-A, which is what you expect from an undersized, teenage defensive wizard. David Eckstein played in 1,311 big-league games. ⓧ **Greg Deichmann** suffered an early-season wrist injury, which makes it hard to judge his results at High-A even after he did come back. A power-hitting right fielder lives within him. ⓧ **Jeremy Eierman** was the 70th overall pick last year as a major-college, power-speed shortstop, though he's probably a power-hitting third baseman long term if he's anything. His brother Johnny washed out after three rookie-ball seasons despite being a Rays third-round pick, if you need another reminder that "if he's anything" is a huge mountain to climb. ⓧ **Jameson Hannah** is a lefty outfielder who the A's took in the second round last year. His speed should keep him in center field, which is where his power profile also belongs. ⓧ **Chris Herrmann** is a fine baseball player with underrated athleticism and defensive utility. He deserves better than a pithy comment in this space. If he didn't then why would his name not literally be German for "Mr. Man?" ⓧ **Corban Joseph** has been in organized baseball for the past ten years, and in that span, he has a grand total of 26 major-league plate appearances. Based on his pattern, look for his next appearance in the 2024 Annual. ⓧ It's not clear whether **Bruce Maxwell** lost his presumptive 2018 starting catcher job *because* he pointed a gun at a delivery person over the winter, but it's hard to believe it wasn't on Oakland's mind when Jonathan Lucroy was still available early in the spring. In any event, Maxwell shouldn't even be a starter on a bad team, much less a good one. ⓧ **Kevin Merrell** runs like the dickens, but he hits like the mckittrick ros. ⓧ **Cliff Pennington** is winding down his surprisingly long, solid career as a light-hitting, good-glove infielder after spending most of 2018 struggling in the minors while failing to top 150 plate appearances in the majors for the first time since 2008. ⓧ **Josh Phegley** doesn't hit, catch or stay healthy, and such small portions! (We know he's #actually quite large, don't @ us.) ⓧ **Tyler Ramirez**'s on-base ability should get him some big-league time, and soon, but his corner defensive profile and doubles power mark him as an up-and-down guy, not a true fourth outfielder. Guys like this used to have the careers that now go to extra pitchers. ⓧ **Beau Taylor** is a catcher who stands on the left side, so he'll get as many chances on minor-league deals as he wants even though he can't really hit. He's in this book for the first and perhaps last time because he made a brief big-league debut last year and notched a double and a walk, which puts him three bases up on the lot of youse.

Pitchers

PITCHER	TEAM	LVL	AGE	W	L	SV	G	GS	IP	H	HR	BB/9	K/9	K	GB%	WHIP	ERA	DRA	WARP
Tanner Anderson	IND	AAA	25	3	2	6	39	0	61^1	65	2	2.2	7.2	49	63%	1.30	2.64	4.11	0.7
	PIT	MLB	25	1	0	0	6	0	11^1	15	1	6.4	4.8	6	58%	2.03	6.35	6.40	-0.2
Paul Blackburn	OAK	MLB	24	2	3	0	6	6	27^2	33	2	2.0	6.2	19	48%	1.41	7.16	3.88	0.5
Parker Bridwell	SLC	AAA	26	1	1	0	6	6	28	50	4	2.9	6.1	19	38%	2.11	8.68	9.36	-1.2
	ANA	MLB	26	1	0	0	5	1	6^2	14	5	2.7	4.1	3	36%	2.40	17.55	4.61	0.0
Aaron Brooks	CSP	AAA	28	9	4	0	26	15	99^1	100	8	2.5	6.7	74	56%	1.29	3.35	4.68	0.9
	OAK	MLB	28	0	0	0	3	0	2^2	1	0	6.8	3.4	1	71%	1.12	0.00	4.72	0.0
Ryan Dull	NAS	AAA	28	3	2	1	23	0	28	27	5	2.6	11.6	36	45%	1.25	3.54	2.86	0.7
	OAK	MLB	28	0	0	0	28	0	25^1	22	3	2.5	7.5	21	35%	1.14	4.26	3.83	0.3
Parker Dunshee	STO	A+	23	6	2	0	12	10	70	61	7	2.2	10.5	82	35%	1.11	2.70	4.07	1.0
	MID	AA	23	7	4	0	12	12	80^2	59	5	1.6	9.0	81	34%	0.90	2.01	3.52	1.7
Brady Feigl	VER	A-	22	1	1	0	8	5	20	6	0	3.2	12.1	27	59%	0.65	1.35	3.50	0.4
	BLT	A	22	0	1	0	3	3	6	5	1	1.5	10.5	7	56%	1.00	3.00	2.68	0.2
Dean Kiekhefer	PEN	AA	29	0	0	0	8	0	8	7	0	1.1	11.2	10	45%	1.00	1.12	4.22	0.1
	NAS	AAA	29	8	1	0	32	1	44^2	50	4	1.2	7.3	36	54%	1.25	3.83	3.03	1.1
	OAK	MLB	29	0	0	0	4	0	2	7	1	4.5	4.5	1	67%	4.00	18.00	3.81	0.0
J.B. Wendelken	MID	AA	25	0	1	3	11	0	13^1	11	3	6.8	15.5	23	43%	1.58	3.38	2.78	0.3
	NAS	AAA	25	1	1	3	22	1	35^1	29	2	2.5	13.2	52	49%	1.10	2.80	1.72	1.4
	OAK	MLB	25	0	0	0	13	0	16^2	8	1	2.7	7.6	14	40%	0.78	0.54	4.16	0.1

The Pirates featured an all-Ivy League battery four times in September, with

Tanner Anderson (Harvard) pitching to Ryan Lavarnway (Yale). Rumors that scientists were working to harness this smart battery in an attempt to reduce worldwide energy use and global emissions could not be confirmed. ⚾ **Paul Blackburn** was healthy only for a month last season, sandwiched between a forearm strain to start the year and tennis elbow to end it, though neither required surgery. He's still just 25 and remains a solid back-of-the-rotation option if he can stay on the mound. ⚾ A double-digit ERA never feels good, even when it was a ludicrously small sample size in an injury-ravaged season. **Parker Bridwell**'s elbow kept him out of four months (and didn't look quite right after that) but none of that matters to his baseball card, which will display that 17.55 for as long as he's in production. ⚾ **Aaron Brooks** doesn't miss enough bats to pitch in the big leagues, which may not prevent him from being Oakland's fourth starter in 2019. ⚾ **Jharel Cotton** entered spring training last year hoping to prove he belongs in the majors after a miserable 2017; instead, he had Tommy John surgery in late March. ⚾ **Ryan Dull** is an undersized slider artist whose spring shoulder strain and rough May took him out of the A's bullpen mix. His final season line contained a critical drop in strikeout rate, reflecting a substantially more hittable slider that will need to regain its previous form to make him a middle-relief option going forward. ⚾ **Parker "Crocodile" Dunshee** spent 2018 doing what he did in 2017: out-pitching his lack of stuff by changing speeds and throwing strikes, this time up to a successful half-season at Double-A. On a Pitching Staff of the Future, he could throw 150 solid frames without ever sniffing the first or seventh inning. ⚾ **Brady Feigl** is in this book to ensure that you Google his name and marvel at the weirdness of his simultaneous existence with the Brady Feigl in the Rangers' minor-league system. We're not living in a sophisticated simulation run by some unfathomable higher power; we're living in a beta test. ⚾ **Daulton Jefferies** missed essentially all of 2017–2018 after Tommy John surgery, but threw in instructional league and is expected to start 2019 in full health. Who knows what the lost development time will cost him, but he had a mid-rotation ceiling once upon a time. ⚾ **James Kaprielian**'s upside is worth more than 41 words in this book, but 29 regular-season innings since being drafted in 2015 (and 27 more in the Arizona Fall League) means there's simply no data. Dammit, Jim, we're baseball analysts, not doctors. ⚾ Run-of-the-mill lefty reliever **Dean Kiekhefer** has the name of a man who belongs in Cooperstown and the strikeout rate of a man who belongs in Triple-A. ⚾ **J.B. Wendelken** probably pitch in middle relief with a 95 mph fastball, but **J.B. Wendelken**'t be counted on for much more than that.

Athletics Prospects

The State of the System:
It feels like a better system that it actually is since most of the pitchers are hurt and one of the toolsy outfielders is actually a football player.

The Top Ten:

1   **Jesus Luzardo   LHP**   OFP: 70   Likely: 60   ETA: 2019
Born: 09/30/97   Age: 21   Bats: L   Throws: L   Height: 6'1"   Weight: 205
Origin: Round 3, 2016 Draft (#94 overall)

The Report: Luzardo is one of the most polished and skilled pitchers you'll see in the minor leagues. He has a relatively short pitcher's frame and doesn't have overly long levers, but is a plus athlete with quality quick twitch and coordination. He has very clean arm action and while his delivery can be a bit rotational, he has no trouble repeating his release point. He sits 93-95 with the four-seam fastball and has average command of the offering. His primary secondary is a plus 85-86 changeup with good arm speed, tumble, and some fade. Luzardo was obviously working on finding consistency with his breaking ball in the two starts I saw him, but the 82-84 curve flashed plus multiple times, with plus depth and spin. The pitch has both vertical and horizontal break when located at the knees or higher, but the bottom drops out when he throws it below the zone.

Luzardo also showed impressive pitchability, as he was comfortable using his breaking ball early in counts to surprise the hitter for an easy strike one. He threw his changeup sparingly and was able to get hitters to whiff just by locating his fastball and breaking ball.

Luzardo profiles as a No. 3 starter on a first division team with a real possibility at being one of the better pitchers in the game if his command develops further.

The Risks: Medium. The risk is about as low as it gets for pitchers who have already had UCL trouble. He has great feel for two of his three plus offerings, and average command. He's ready for the big leagues, and as his body finishes maturing and he gains experience, his command and feel should get even better.

Ben Carsley's Fantasy Take: For my money, Luzardo is the second-best pitching prospect in the game, trailing only Forrest Whitley. In the top-101 I compared him to the best version of James Paxton, and I truly believe that's his upside. Sure, he already has TJ on his resume, but he's far removed from the procedure and clearly hasn't suffered from it. Luzardo is a top-20 overall fantasy prospect and a stud in the making. I expect him to serve as a fantasy SP2/3 for as long as he's healthy.

2 **A.J. Puk   LHP**   OFP: 60   Likely: 50   ETA: 2020
Born: 04/25/95   Age: 24   Bats: L   Throws: L   Height: 6'7"   Weight: 220
Origin: Round 1, 2016 Draft (#6 overall)

The Report: There's an alternate timeline where Puk doesn't blow out his UCL last spring and carves up the minors on the way to a fabulous late-season debut and Wild Card game start. Despite their surprise 2018 playoff run, the A's might have preferred that fork in the multiverse as well, as they enter 2019 with Yusmeiro Petit among their best five starting options. But you can't change the past—even if you have Jose Canseco's time machine—and pitchers of all stripes break. Puk won't be ready for Opening Day 2019, but you should see him sometime in the summer.

Before the injury the stuff was, well, good enough to rank Puk as a top 30 prospect in baseball. He hits the mid-90s—sometimes higher—from the left side with premium extension and deception, a slider that looked like a potential 7 on its good days—and mechanical issues that left him struggling at times to throw enough strikes. The stuff was good enough that it didn't really matter in the minors, but we will have to see how much of it comes back from surgery. (Anecdotally, I tend to be more concerned about the "bad mechanics" dudes coming back, but that's a personal predilection with no real science backing it). There was always a fair bit of reliever risk in the profile, but with that two-pitch combo, Puk would have closer stuff.

The Risks: High. Puk is coming off Tommy John surgery and has missed significant, important development time. We won't really know what he is now until he steps on a mound in Arizona sometime this summer. If you want to look at positive variance this could easily be a 70/50 if you were so inclined.

Ben Carsley's Fantasy Take: As we've preached many, many times, the no. 1 thing dynasty leaguers should be looking for in their pitching prospects is strikeouts. That makes Puk perhaps an even better fantasy prospect than IRL one, as he should routinely strike out more than a batter per inning in whatever capacity he pitches. Is the dream that he morphs into a high-strikeout, tolerable-WHIP pitcher, a la Patrick Corbin? Yes. But even if he as to move to the bullpen, Puk could have Andrew Miller's career. That'd make him ownable in the vast majority of leagues even if he wasn't a closer.

3 **Sean Murphy   C**   OFP: 60   Likely: 50   ETA: Late 2019
Born: 10/10/94   Age: 24   Bats: R   Throws: R   Height: 6'3"   Weight: 215
Origin: Round 3, 2016 Draft (#83 overall)

The Report: Murphy is the best defender among the top tier catching prospects in baseball right now. He flashes a plus-plus arm and is an athletic backstop who draws raves for his receiving and staff management already. There are minor durability concerns, as he's missed time with a broken hamate in both 2016 and 2018, but those tend to be more freakish type things, and he doesn't have a third one to break anyway.

As a potential 70-grade defender behind the plate, Murphy won't have to hit much to be a major-league regular. He has plus raw power in his locker though, and has had some success getting to it in games (it's worth mentioning that he's generally been old for the level at his minor-league stops). The swing is a bit stiff, although that has manifested more in poor quality of contact than swing-and-miss so far. But even with a below-average hit tool and average pop, Murphy's glove is good enough to make him a solid regular. Anything past that, and he could play in a few all-star games.

The Risks: Medium. It would be low, but catchers are weird, and Murphy keeps breaking his hamate bone. The defensive profile should be good enough to keep him employed in the fraternal order of backup catchers for a decade even if he doesn't really hit.

Ben Carsley's Fantasy Take: You should stay away from catching prospects in general in dynasty leagues. Glove-first catching prospects? That's a hard no. Murphy may be of interest in AL-only squads once he starts playing, but he lacks the upside to routinely perform as a top 12-or-so option at the position. And given the state of the position, that's saying something.

4

Kyler Murray   OF   OFP: 70   Likely: 60   ETA: NFL - September 2019
Born: 08/07/97   Age: 21   Bats: R   Throws: R   Height: 5'11"   Weight: 195
Origin: Round 1, 2018 Draft (#9 overall)

The Report: Murray originally signed with Texas A&M out of high school as a five-star quarterback recruit, and was widely regarded as the best prep football player in the country. He platooned for the Aggies in 2015 as a true freshman before transferring to Oklahoma where he initially played sparingly behind Baker Mayfield. Murray won a 2018 camp battle to claim Oklahoma's starting role after reaching a deal with the A's to play his redshirt junior football season while under a baseball contract. He proceeded to have one of the best seasons in college football history, usurping Alabama quarterback Tua Tagovailoa for the Heisman Trophy, and leading Oklahoma to the Orange Bowl.

Meanwhile, Murray had a parallel career in baseball. He was also considered a first-round MLB Draft prospect out of high school, but removed his name from the draft pool entirely. He didn't play baseball at all at A&M, but did join the Sooners as a sophomore in 2017. He scuffled badly initially, and scuffled some more in the Cape Cod League that summer. But then he had a brilliant junior campaign, establishing himself once more as a top baseball player for his class as an athletic five-tool center field prospect. This time he was interested in a career on the diamond, and the A's drafted him ninth overall and signed him for $4.66 million, only very slightly below slot value.

Despite his recruiting pedigree, Murray was not considered a particularly great NFL quarterback prospect until this past fall, which was why the A's felt reasonably secure drafting him in the top ten and letting him play an additional season of football. He's small—quarterbacks generally have to be over six feet to be high draft picks—and he just hadn't played enough in college to overcome the height issue perception. But the NFL is changing to a quick passing, dynamic offensive league built around run/pass options and space plays, and Murray is a perfect fit for the new wave of football. Mayfield made a similar late rise in Lincoln Riley's system at Oklahoma, and he exploded on the NFL scene in 2018. Combine all that with a weak quarterback class, and all of a sudden Murray is the talk of the gridiron in a way Oakland couldn't have expected when drafting him.

We're reading tea leaves here, but it seems more likely at this moment in time that he's going to play professional football—and only professional football—moving forward.

The Risks: So yeah, we ranked Kyler Murray as the 101st best prospect in baseball. The list locked for book publication literally the day of the Orange Bowl. At the time, he was still committed to baseball, and we do tend to reserve the 101st spot for the most *interesting* OFP 60 type who didn't make the top 100 proper.

In the month-plus since, Murray has publicly wavered on which sport he'd play, declared for the NFL Draft, failed to come to a new contractual agreement with the Athletics, and is poised to go at or near the top of a second sport's draft. He was already interesting and he's become far more interesting, but not in the way you want if you have a vested interest in seeing him play baseball. He might still play baseball, if not immediately than perhaps down the road. He might even try to play both eventually, and if he was somehow successful at *that*, he'd be the biggest star in sports.

Football jokes aside, we'd rate Murray as a high risk OFP 60/Likely 50 as a baseball prospect. That's akin to Travis Swaggerty, a top 101 guy with a similar toolsy college outfielder profile who went right after him in last summer's draft. He has all the baseball tools you'd expect from a guy who went in the top ten despite all the risk involved, though he's raw due to lack of reps. We're just not convinced he's going to pick baseball anymore, which is a risk so big that it is basically all that's worth talking about.

Ben Carsley's Fantasy Take: He'd be a top-60ish prospect if we knew he was committed to baseball, but it sure seems like he's not committed to baseball. Do with that information what you will.

5. Lazaro Armenteros OF
OFP: 60 Likely: 50 ETA: 2021
Born: 05/22/99 Age: 20 Bats: R Throws: R Height: 6'0" Weight: 182
Origin: International Free Agent, 2016

The Report: Two months into the season, Lazarito looked like a sure shot 2019 Top 101 name. A polished outfielder with potential plus hit and power tools off to a good start in full-season ball at 19? Yes please. Even after a quad injury cost him a month, he made the honorable mentions for the midseason 50.

Lazarito was a mess after coming back from his injury, so we are cooling our jets a little bit. While he didn't quite look one hundred percent in the late summer, we don't foresee any long term effects here. Given that he's a far from a sure shot to stick up the middle, any lower body injuries are going to be a little concerning though, especially since his below-average arm would force him to left.

You're buying the bat here anyway, and despite a toe tap and leg kick for timing, Lazarito has fluid, well-balanced hitting mechanics married to a good approach and above-average barrel control. The plus power is mostly theoretical at this point, but the swing has some loft, and you'd expect him to add strength in his twenties. It wasn't quite the breakout season we expected around Memorial Day, but it's also hard to quibble with the overall performance from a teenager in the Midwest League. So while we aren't firing the afterburners quite yet, we'll keep the engine running.

The Risks: High. He's more polished than toolsy, although the tools aren't bad at all. He's also got half an injury-marred A-ball season under his belt, and he may have to slide to left field.

Ben Carsley's Fantasy Take: Lazarito didn't make it onto our top-101, but he'd be among the next 50 names. A healthy campaign where he holds his own against better competition could see Armenteros make a sizable jump up our rankings, however, and he's a good one to try to buy low on if someone else in your league is out of patience. A future as an OF3 is still in play, albeit perhaps less likely than an OF4/5 outcome.

6. Austin Beck OF
OFP: 60 Likely: 45 ETA: 2022
Born: 11/21/98 Age: 20 Bats: R Throws: R Height: 6'1" Weight: 200
Origin: Round 1, 2017 Draft (#6 overall)

The Report: Beck played well in the Midwest League last summer, looking every bit like the toolsy athlete the A's envisioned when they popped him with the sixth overall pick in the 2017 draft. He made great strides at the plate, cleaning up his approach and reducing his strikeout rate. He still tends to chase breaking stuff but he adjusts well and has enough barrel control to project an average hit tool. He's more of a doubles hitter than a true power threat at this point, but his plus raw will eventually play in games. Quick and athletic, he's a plus runner who plays a quality centerfield. His instincts are sound and he's got enough arm for right field if needed.

There's still no guarantee Beck hits upper-level arms, but he's off to a good start. There's plenty of upside remaining too, but to reach his ceiling as a first division centerfielder, he'll need to get more of his raw power into games.

The Risks: High. He's still very raw and has yet to face pitching above Low A.

Ben Carsley's Fantasy Take: I considered Beck toward the end of my personal top-101, and I think it's safe to say he's a top-125-ish prospect at this point. You sort of wish that one out of his ETA, floor, or ceiling was more fantasy-friendly, but at the end of the day there's still the makings of a very solid all-around fantasy OF3 here if it all clicks. If Beck performs well against tougher pitching, it's easy to imagine him being a borderline top-50 guy a year from now.

7. Grant Holmes   RHP   OFP: 55   Likely: 40
ETA: Late 2019 or early 2020, health permitting
Born: 03/22/96   Age: 23   Bats: L   Throws: R   Height: 6'1"   Weight: 215
Origin: Round 1, 2014 Draft (#22 overall)

The Report: I've been a fan of Holmes since his draft year, and it isn't just the plus-plus flow. He's never quite fully broken out, but looked well on his way to being a useful major-league arm by the close of the 2017 season. And hey, he was 21 and had a year of moderate Double-A success under his belt. Maybe 2018 would be the year he broke out?

Instead, 2018 was the year he broke; pitchers, man. Holmes missed almost the full season with a rotator cuff injury. No one will confuse me with a doctor, but I believe that's connected to the shoulder, and you don't need to be a doctor to know that shoulder injuries for pitchers are, uh, bad. Very bad.

When he did toe the rubber, the stuff looked more or less like it did in 2017: fastball up to 95, potential plus breaker, but six inning samples aren't gonna keep you in a meaningful spot on a team's prospect list. Amazingly though, he's not even the riskiest or the least healthy arm on this list. Pitchers, man.

The Risks: Extreme. The stuff looked fine in his brief post-rotator-cuff-issue appearances, but uh he also missed most of the year with a shoulder injury, so…

Ben Carsley's Fantasy Take: Holmes used to be a bit of a BP Fantasy Team favorite, but at this point there's relatively little that distinguishes him from the myriad backend/spot fantasy starter types who litter these lists… except for a shoulder injury. Unless you roster 200-plus prospects Holmes can be and should already have been dropped.

8. James Kaprielian RHP   OFP: 55   Likely: 40
ETA: 2019, if you feel like gambling he's healthy
Born: 03/02/94   Age: 25   Bats: R   Throws: R   Height: 6'4"   Weight: 200
Origin: Round 1, 2015 Draft (#16 overall)

The Report: It's been over 33 months since Kaprielian last took the mound in a regular-season game. He missed most of 2016 with flexor problems, but came back and was fantastically impressive in the Arizona Fall League, with a big velocity spike causing his perceived upside to jump substantially—enough that he climbed into our top 101 that winter. He arrived in camp with the wind at his back and a chance to rocket through New York's farm system and… immediately blew out his UCL.

He was included in the Sonny Gray trade while rehabbing, and was expected to return to game action by midseason as an Oakland farmhand. He didn't return at all, with a troubled rehab plagued by shoulder injuries, although he was throwing during instructs. He's going to (hopefully) return in 2019 as a 25-year-old with 56 1/3 innings, all in the low-minors or the AFL, and all in 2015 and 2016.

The last time we saw Kaprielian toe the rubber regularly, he possessed top-of-the-rotation stuff: four pitches that projected above-average, led with a fastball sitting 94-97 and touching 99. Obviously, we have utterly no idea whether he can recapture that form, or maintain it in any type of regular pitching role. But it was good enough that he landed as the 58th best prospect in baseball back then, despite missing six months with a known Tommy John surgery precursor. It was good enough that he was a key part of a major trade while hurt. It was good enough that two years later, after a troubled rehab and without ever throwing a real pitch in their system, the A's added him to the 40-man roster. And it was good enough that we're still ranking him today.

The Risks: As extreme as anyone in baseball. Our dearly departed leader Craij (RIP Craij) used Kaprielian as the example of players for whom the beta was so high that the role grades undershot the risk last spring, and that was before he missed *another* season. He could be in the majors in a few months if he's healthy; he might also never throw a pitch in the upper-minors.

Ben Carsley's Fantasy Take: I tend not to shy away from injury-prone pitchers if I think they possess big-time upside (hello, Nate Pearson), but Kaprielian is a bridge too far for me. He's a top-200 dude because there just aren't many guys who can match his pure strikeout potential, but he didn't sniff our top-101 and I don't think he'd sniff a theoretical top-150 either. I am too scared.

9. Jorge Mateo SS   OFP: 50   Likely: 40   ETA: Late 2019
Born: 06/23/95   Age: 24   Bats: R   Throws: R   Height: 6'0"   Weight: 190
Origin: International Free Agent, 2012

The Report: Mateo is one of the fastest players in the minors. He's a premium athlete, full stop. He can play shortstop, center field, and second base, and presumably would be fine at the positions down the defensive spectrum from there. At times, he's shown real flashes of power, and he wound up with 60 extra base hits in the minors in 2017.

At the end of the day though, you can't steal first base. Mateo hit .230 last year, in the PCL of all places. He's not going to put together enough walks or power to make up for that level of bad hitting, and indeed the collapse in hitting ability torpedoed his non-speed secondary offensive skills too. In sum, he had a 58 DRC+ in Triple-A, worse than any regular hitter in the majors except for Chris Davis.

We've had concerns about Mateo's ability to hit for average since basically day one. He has good technical underpinnings in terms of swing plane, bat speed, and bat control, which has led to sporadic bursts of success at the plate. Unfortunately, his plate discipline and pitch recognition often limits him far more than it should. Those concerns were amplified when he spent a year-and-a-half puttering in High-A, and remain significant today.

Mateo is still likely to have a substantial MLB career if things don't work out with the stick, as his speed and defense will give him enough utility to survive in a bench role. But it might not be as a particularly valuable player unless he figures out a way to get to first. We might even suggest the Baltimore chop at this point.

The Risks: Medium, almost all in the overall offensive profile. Speed is a useful tool, but hit is more useful, and Mateo has only consistently shown the former.

Ben Carsley's Fantasy Take: We used to be pretty high on Mateo, but he has proven fairly definitively to us that he can't hit enough for his speed to matter. If you want to call him a top-200 guy because of the pure speed upside that's fine, but I've cut bait pretty much everywhere I held him at this point. If he ends up playing near-every day at some point due to injuries or small steps forward in his bat, then sure, pick him up again. But Mateo looks like a bench piece through and through.

10 Jameson Hannah OF

OFP: 50   Likely: 40   ETA: 2021
Born: 08/10/97   Age: 21   Bats: L   Throws: L   Height: 5'9"   Weight: 185
Origin: Round 2, 2018 Draft (#50 overall)

The Report: Hannah played on a high-powered offense at Dallas Baptist and was pretty clearly the best player on the team due to his bat and ability in center. He is a plus athlete with good coordination and quick twitch. He has broad shoulders and an athletic build on a short frame that doesn't have much room, if any, to put on weight without losing a step.

Hannah has above-average feel for the barrel and plus bat speed, but his swing generates his hardest contact on low line drives and burners. His average raw power gets left by the wayside in most plate appearances. Hannah is willing to take walks, but struggles with the soft stuff.

Hannah is currently a plus runner and he gets down the line very quickly from the left side. His jumps in center and plus footspeed give him plenty of range, although he will need to clean up his routes and reads to get the most out of his wheels. Hannah's arm is fringy and will likely play best in left or center.

Hannah's athleticism and tools suggest a future as a versatile fourth outfielder who can get on base at a decent clip. If he can tap into more of his raw power without losing a step, he could play himself into regular work in center.

The Risks: Medium: Still far away and although the athleticism, feel for hit, and current approach suggest he will transition well into his first full season of pro ball, he struggled in the Cape against high level pitching.

Ben Carsley's Fantasy Take: Hannah is the type of guy who may end up on the very back of a top-101 the year before he reaches the majors if we think he has a clear path to playing time. But that's his ceiling, and given the likelihood that he ends up more of a good fourth outfielder than a true first division dude, he's just one for the watch list for now.

The Next Five

11 **Nick Allen SS**
Born: 10/08/98   Age: 20   Bats: R   Throws: R   Height: 5'9"   Weight: 155
Origin: Round 3, 2017 Draft (#81 overall)

12 **Kevin Merrell SS**
Born: 12/14/95   Age: 23   Bats: L   Throws: R   Height: 6'1"   Weight: 180
Origin: Round 1, 2017 Draft (#33 overall)

About as good a matched pair as you will find back-to-back in any system (although Holmes/Kaprielian aren't far off I suppose).

When the Athletics spent two million bucks in the 2017 draft to buy the diminutive Allen out of his USC commitment, they were purchasing a glove and some speed with the hopes that the bat would develop. He struggled some in an aggressive Midwest League assignment, and it remains hard to see much impact with the bat, but the glove and speed were as advertised. He's strong for his size but this is a gap power profile at best. Allen doesn't have to hit a ton to be a second-division starter type, but the most likely outcome here is speedy utility infielder.

Merrell is the Cal League version of Allen. He's faster by a fair bit, as he'll pop borderline elite run times, but is a bit rougher at the six. He's improved enough that we'll project him as a shortstop though, and he's a more polished hitter—as you'd expect from the college bat versus the prep one. He doesn't offer much in the way of pop either, as he's slight of frame with a relatively flat swing plane and little leg drive. If he slaps enough balls into the alleys and sneaks some extra bases he could play everyday, but again, the most likely outcome here is (very) speedy utility infielder.

13 Jeremy Eierman SS
Born: 09/10/96   Age: 22   Bats: R   Throws: R   Height: 6'1"   Weight: 205
Origin: Round 2, 2018 Draft (#70 overall)

Eierman certainly has more power than the two shortstops ahead of him on this list, but that comes with a price. The swing is long and leveraged, and he tends to take hacks more appropriate for a more stoutly built baseball player. So while he offers plus raw power, how much of it plays in games against better arms is far from determined. He's also less likely to stick at short than Allen or Merrell. I'm happy to write off a poor post-draft performance, even for a polished college performer in the Penn League—it's a long season for those dudes—but it reflects some of the offensive concerns that cropped up his junior year at Missouri State and slid him down everyone's draft board. There's certainly enough power potential here to project a second division starter in the middle infield, but again, the most likely outcome here is utility infielder.

14 Daulton Jefferies RHP
Born: 08/02/95   Age: 23   Bats: L   Throws: R   Height: 6'0"   Weight: 180
Origin: Round 1, 2016 Draft (#37 overall)

The last two spots on the top 15 are injury mulligans, which isn't a great sign for your system depth after you had three (arguably three and a half) in your top ten as well. Jefferies is of the more traditional variety, as he spent almost all of 2018 recovering from Tommy John surgery. There were already questions coming out of college about whether his short, slight frame would hold up to the rigors of pro starting, and he has answered exactly none of them two-and-a-half years into his career. He's shown three average-or-better offerings in the past, and Oakland must be getting awfully tempted to turn him loose in the pen. The problem is that Jefferies really needs pro reps. It's easier to get those when you are stretched out, so you might as well give him one more spin as a starter, even if "fastball/slider reliever" looks like his destiny.

15 Greg Deichmann OF
Born: 05/31/95   Age: 24   Bats: L   Throws: R   Height: 6'2"   Weight: 190
Origin: Round 2, 2017 Draft (#43 overall)

You can explain away some of Deichmann's struggles this year to the wrist injury that limited him to just 58 games, but you still have to reckon with the fact that a 23-year-old corner outfielder posted a .667 OPS in the Cal League. The tools are there for a power-hitting right fielder, but the wrist injury can't explain away the issues with north-south sequencing or spin. Ultimately, his season was too muddled to write Deichmann off entirely, but it's also a lost year of needed development time and he'll be under a lot of pressure to hit this season.

Top Talents 25 and Under (born 4/1/93 or later)

1. Matt Chapman
2. Jesus Luzardo
3. Matt Olson
4. Ramon Laureano
5. A.J. Puk
6. Sean Murphy
7. Franklin Barreto
8. Dustin Fowler
9. Daniel Mengden
10. Frankie Montas

Well hello there, beautiful. This crew suddenly harkens back to the halcyon days of the early aughts in terms of both quality and quantity of controllable young talent in, or at the cusp of, the big leagues. And it doesn't include recent acquisition and former undisputed champion uber-prospect Jurickson Profar, who aged out of consideration by mere weeks.

Matt Chapman introduced himself to the world last year, bringing his elite leather and game power to bear on American League opponents for a full season. Sure, he'll likely continue to whiff a good bit, and his lack of barrel control may prevent him from becoming a true superstar. But the Fullerton product sure looks like a swell bet to get awfully close and he's set to be one of the game's best players for the next several years.

For his part, Matt Olson followed up a dynamite debut with some expected offensive regression in Year Two. The power is very real though, and the glove looks pretty sweet by cold-corner standards as well. It's certainly not the most dynamic of profiles, and he's never going to win a stolen base title. But a solid two-to-three win first baseman with 30ish bankable dingers remains a very nice thing for a cost-conscious team to be able to bank.

Ramon Laureano introduced himself to the world when he uncorked one of the best throws of the year, but he's looked like a solid all-around ballplayer for much longer than that. A down first half in 2017 took some of the shine off his Lancaster breakout the year before, but he went right on back to hitting at Double-A that summer and hasn't really stopped since. An electric defensive package, strong on-base skills and hard line-drive contact… that's a lot of boxes checked for a potential top-of-the-lineup anchor for years to come.

Barreto made our 101 for four consecutive years from 2015 to 2018, but his stock is down after struggling to make quality contact in his first few big-league cameos. That's not great news for a player whose profile has ostensibly rested on the back of a quality hit tool projection. But he's added a good deal of pop to the package, and the athleticism up the middle remains an asset, albeit on the right side of the second-base bag these days.

Dustin Fowler's gruesome knee injury continues to fade further into the rearview mirror, and while he went the Barreto route and struggled to adapt to life in The Show last year, he raked in Triple-A while also logging the top recorded 90-foot sprint speed in the big leagues. He's a highly aggressive hitter, and that's always going to be a limiting factor for his offensive ceiling. But he's a good enough bat-to-ball guy that it can work, and he profiles as a big-league regular.

Daniel Mengden and Frankie Montas did eerily similar work last season, swinging between the rotation and middle relief to provide wonderfully cheap and useful innings despite not striking anybody out. Neither managed to crack six whiffs per nine, and neither in turn cracked 120 for a DRA-. It's unclear where either finds a next gear, though Mengden's hook and Montas' four-seam heat are both legitimate weapons. The important thing is that both managed to defy their peripherals and establish themselves as legitimate big-league arms.

Part 3: Featured Articles

The Hole in The Shift is Fixing Itself

Russell Carleton

I've been on a bit of a mission against The Shift of late. I'm not out to get The Shift for the usual reasons that people oppose it. The words "the right way to play the game" won't be found on my lips. If a team wants to pursue a strategy that is within the rules and it works, then by all means, they have my blessing (not that they need it). Instead, my concern with The Shift is a worry that it doesn't work, or at least that it has a flaw that needs fixing.

The data show that while The Shift does a decent job of preventing singles on balls in play (what it's supposed to do), it also increases the number of walks that happen in front of it, and the number of additional walks outweighs the number of singles saved. It's a problem because you can't throw a guy out if he gets to walk to first base.

But the "why" was important. It seemed that The Shift was changing the way in which pitchers pitched. We saw that there were fewer fastballs thrown in front of The Shift than we might otherwise expect, and that pitchers tended to stay out of the strike zone a little more. Not by a lot. In fact, it might not even be visible to the naked eye. The percentage of pitches that are out of the zone goes from 51.0 to 53.3 from a standard defense (two right/two left) to a full shift (three on one side). That difference stands up even after we control for the types of hitters that get shifted against. And it's enough to drive up the walk rate to where it cancels out the benefits that teams thought they were getting with The Shift… and then some.

But there was some hope. I found that when individual pitchers stayed closer to the in-zone/out-of-zone mix that they used without The Shift on, they could still get the benefits of The Shift without the walk problems. So, in theory, a team could simply figure out a way to convince its pitchers to not fall prey to the walk trap and The Shift would once again be their friend.

It's reasonable to think that some teams might be more hip to this idea than others. Maybe some figured it out a year before the others. Maybe they were better at getting the message across to their pitchers. Or, maybe no one has figured it out yet.

Warning! Gory Mathematical Details Ahead!

I used data from 2015-2017, made available through MLB's data portal, Baseball Savant. They are kind enough to note when teams are using an infield shift (three fielders on one side of second base), as opposed to a "strategic shift" (someone's playing a bit out of position, but it's not quite that drastic) or a "standard" alignment.

Since we're doing this by team, I can't just look at raw walk rates, because we know that some teams have good pitchers and others have not-so-good pitchers. Some have a mix of both. I used the log-odds ratio method to take into account a batter's general walking proclivities, and a pitcher's as well, and then shoving them into a binary logistic regression. Then, I asked the computer to generate a specific coefficient for each team's pitchers, for when they went into The Shift and how that affected their walk rate.

Using those coefficients, I was able to project what would happen if a league-average pitcher faced a league-average hitter (which we expect would product a league-average walk rate; from 2015-2017, 7.7 percent of plate appearances ended in a walk) and then just switched his hat. Here's the top five and the bottom five:

Top 5 Teams	Projected Shift Walk Rate	Bottom 5 Teams	Projected Shift Walk Rate
Rockies	6.2%	Rangers	11.2%
Pirates	6.7%	Mets	10.4%
Indians	7.2%	Dodgers	10.2%
Astros	7.3%	Cardinals	9.9%
Braves	7.7%	Tigers	9.7%

There are probably people out there right now trying to figure out what the common thread is among the top and bottom teams. I'm sure, because this is Baseball Prospectus, people are already trying to make the case that sabermetric "early adopters" have some sort of edge here. I think that the more interesting piece is that by the time you get to fifth place in The Shift, we're at league average.

As a sanity check, I examined the issue on a pitch-by-pitch level, looking at how often pitchers threw their pitches in the GameDay strike zone, and again using the same basic methodology and getting team-specific coefficients. The names on the list re-arranged themselves, but the idea was the same, and the two lists correlated with an R of .593.

There's a reason that I don't usually do this type of leaderboard post. I don't really know what the Rockies, Pirates, Indians, Astros, and Braves have in common, or what they have that the bottom five don't. I can put a shrug emoji here and say, "Well, it must be something!" but that seems like a cop-out. Instead, I'd like to present another table and suggest that the table above doesn't even really matter anymore.

Year	League Percent Outside K Zone (Full Shift)	League Percent in K Zone (No Shift)	Difference
2015	54.1%	51.1%	3.0%
2016	53.3%	50.9%	2.4%
2017	52.6%	50.9%	1.7%
2018	52.0%	50.7%	1.3%

The hole in The Shift is fixing itself, and it's coming down really fast league wide. In my earlier work on The Shift, I suggested that until teams stopped having such a huge difference between their out-of-zone rate with and without The Shift on, there would just be too many walks for The Shift to make sense. It seems that all 30 of them have been working toward just that. I once estimated that it takes about 10 years for an idea to filter its way through baseball. At this rate, it looks like teams are going to catch up a lot faster than that. And yeah, they're all saber-smart now.

It's likely that whatever magic it was that the Rockies and Pirates had has made its way to Texas and Queens. Or is at least on its way. And if teams are committing to fixing the walk problem, then it's likely that they will continue shifting and shifting a lot.

And eventually it's going to actually make sense for them to do it.

—*Russell Carleton is a former author of Baseball Prospectus and now an analyst for the New York Mets.*

The State of the Quality Start

Rob Mains

One of the seven things you (probably) didn't know about the 2018 season is that quality starts—defined as a start lasting six or more innings with three or fewer earned runs allowed—as a percentage of total starts cratered to an all-time low of 41 percent. I want to look a little more deeply into this, since it's been a while (May of 2016, to be exact) since I've examined quality starts.

The term *quality start* is credited to *Philadelphia Inquirer* sportswriter John Lowe. It's been derided ever since he coined it in December of 1985. Three runs in six innings? That's a 4.50 ERA! In what world is that a measure of quality?

Let's start with that criticism. It's true that 3 x 9 / 6 = 4.5. (You came here for this sort of high-level math, right?) But it's also true that type of start, meeting the bare minimum for earning a quality start, is unusual. Here's the proportion of quality starts in which the pitcher lasted exactly six innings and yielded exactly three earned runs. (I'm going to confine this analysis to the 30-team era, 1998-present. Almost all data retrieved in this article is via the Baseball-Reference Play Index.)

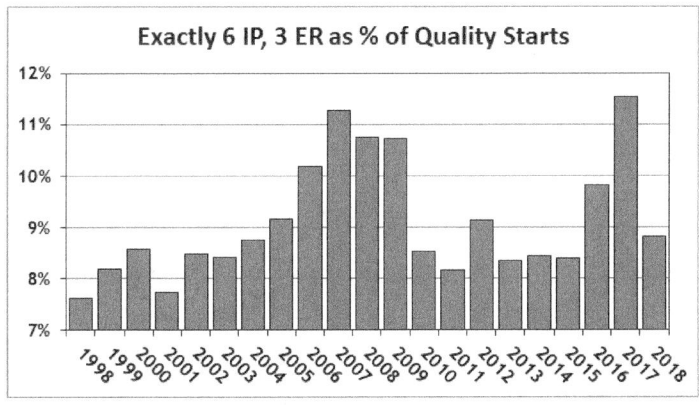

There were 1,997 quality starts in 2018. Only 176, or fewer than one in 11, featured a pitcher going six innings and allowing three earned runs. Put another way, the percentage of quality starts that resulted in a 4.50 ERA (8.8 percent) is less than half the percentage of games in which a batter hit two home runs and his team lost (22.5 percent; 237-69 won-lost). That doesn't impugn hitting two homers.

So if a 4.50 ERA isn't the norm, what is? How good are quality starts?

Pretty good, it turns out. First, on a team level:

Teams receiving a quality start from their pitcher won 68.4 percent of their games in 2018, in line with the 30-team era average of 67.9 percent. A team with a .684 winning percentage wins 111 games. Getting a quality start is definitely a good thing. Individual pitchers throwing quality starts have a higher winning percentage because a big slice of team losses is assigned to a reliever.

If teams do well in quality starts, how well do the starting pitchers do? Again, very well.

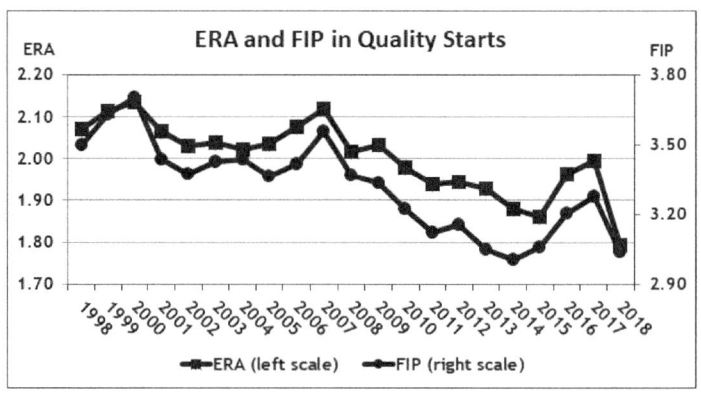

Pitchers in quality starts had a 1.79 ERA (blue line) in 2018, *the lowest in the 30-team era*. Their FIP was higher, 3.04, but still excellent. In the 30-team era, only 2014 had a lower FIP for quality starts, 3.01.

But, of course, the run environment in 2014 was different. Teams in 2014 scored 4.07 runs per game, the fewest in a non-strike year since 1976. They scored 4.45 runs per game in 2018. So surrendering a 3.04 FIP in 2018 is more impressive than 3.01 in 2014. Accordingly, let's look at ERA and FIP in quality starts relative to league averages.

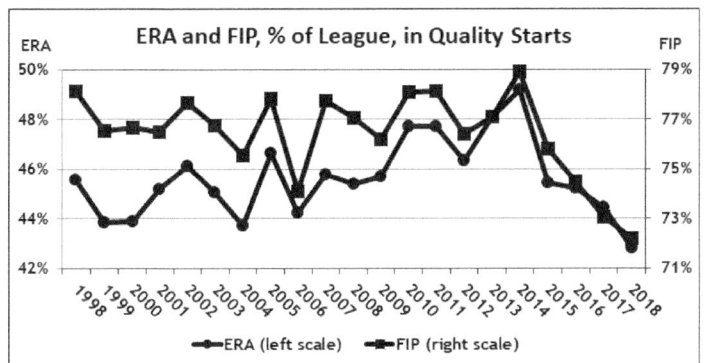

This tells a more dramatic story. Starting pitchers in 2018 gave up a 4.19 ERA and a 4.21 FIP. Starters in quality starts gave up a 1.79 ERA, 43 percent of the league average. Starters in quality starts gave up a 3.04 FIP, 72 percent of the league average. Both of these marks represent lows in the 30-team era.

The takeaway here is this: *Quality starts are better, relative to other starts, than they've ever been over the past 21 years.*

Maybe during the winter I'll look at this over a longer arc of time. For now, though, we can definitively say quality starts are the best they've ever been since the Diamondbacks and Rays joined the majors.

Yet, paradoxically, they're down.

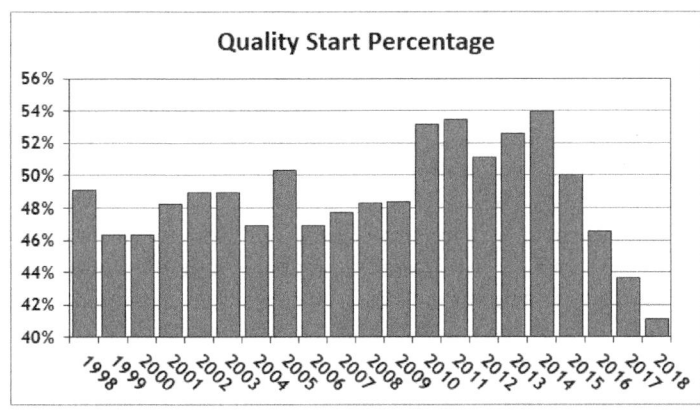

This graph covers only the 30-team era. In my article last week, though, I looked at the years 1908-2018. The result was the same. The 41 percent of starts in 2018 that were quality starts are an all-time low, well below the runners-up: 1930's 43 percent (the year teams scored an all-time record 5.55 runs per game) and last year's 44 percent.

The normal explanation for a dip in quality start percentage is an increase in scoring. When teams score a lot of runs, it's harder for starting pitchers to last six or more innings and limit opponents to three earned runs. From 1998 to 2014, the correlation between runs scored per game and the percentage of starts that were quality starts was -0.94. That means there was an extremely close relationship: More runs, fewer quality starts. Too small a sample? Go back to the start of the Expansion Era, 1961, and the relationship is even more negative, a -0.95 correlation, though 2014.

But that's broken down over the past four years:

- 2015: Runs per game increased from 4.07 to 4.25, quality start percentage decreased from 54.0 to 50.1. Yes, that's a negative relationship, but the regression model would predict a decline of 1.5 percentage points. We got 3.9 instead.
- 2016: Runs per game increased from 4.25 to 4.48, quality start percentage decreased from 50.1 to 46.6. Past experience would suggest a decline of just 1.8 percentage points. We got 3.4.
- 2017: Runs per game increased from 4.48 to 4.65, quality start percentage decreased from 46.6 to 43.6. Again, the direction's right, but the magnitude isn't. Using the relationship from 1998 to 2014, that increase in scoring should've reduced quality starts by 1.3 percentage points, not 2.9.
- 2018: Runs per game declined from 4.65 to 4.45. That should've resulted in the quality start percentage moving in the other direction, rising 1.6 points. It didn't. It fell 2.6 points, as noted, to an all-time low.

Granted, we're talking about just four years here. Maybe they're outliers. But I don't think they are. Quality starts, as noted, are as good or better than ever. But they're rarer than ever as well. And I think I know why.

To get a quality start, you need to allow three or fewer earned and pitch at least six innings. That's 18 outs. Here's a graph showing the number of starting pitchers who limited their opponents to three or fewer earned runs but got pulled after pitching at least five innings but fewer than six:

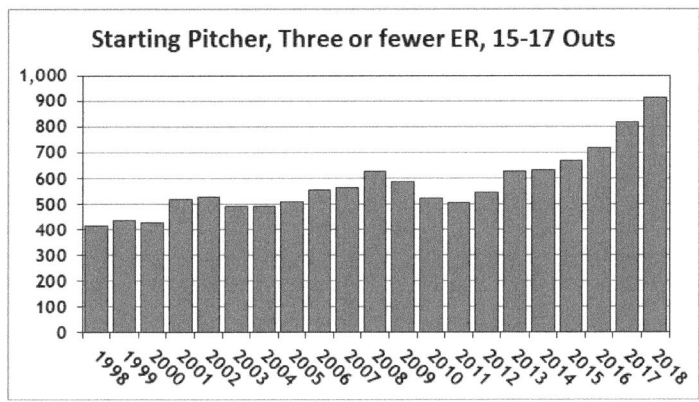

A pitcher getting 15 outs pitched five innings. A pitcher getting 16 outs pitched 5 1/3. A pitcher getting 17 outs pitched 5 2/3. More than ever before, pitchers are being removed from games in which they are within 1-3 outs of a quality start, falling just short of the six-inning finish line. Widespread acknowledgement of the times-through-the-order penalty and a flotilla of available bullpen arms is making the quality start simultaneously both more excellent and more rare.

Which is ironic, given that we saw a new post-war quality start record this season:

Rank	Pitcher	Season	Consecutive QS
1	Jacob deGrom	2018	24
2	Bob Gibson	1968	22
-	Chris Carpenter	2005	22
4	Johan Santana	2004	21
5	Luis Tiant	1968	20
-	Mike Scott	1986	20
-	Jake Arrieta	2015	20
8	Robin Roberts	1952	19
-	Tom Seaver	1973	19
-	Jack Morris	1983	19
-	Greg Maddux	1998	19
-	Josh Johnson	2010	19
-	Jon Lester	2014	19

While there have been longer streaks spread over multiple seasons, no pitcher since World War II threw more consecutive quality starts in one year than Jacob deGrom this year. The fact that he did in a year in which quality starts were the rarest they've ever been adds to the accomplishment.

—*Rob Mains is an author of Baseball Prospectus.*

Heads-Up Hacking—The First Pitch

Matthew Trueblood

Batters fell behind in a higher percentage of all plate appearances in 2018 than in any previous season for which we have pitch-by-pitch data. That kind of granular information goes back only to 1988, but we might safely assume (given all we know about baseball as it had been before that, and as it has been in the years since) that batters have *never* fallen behind at a higher rate than they did last season.

Through the 1990s, the percentage of all plate appearances that began 0-1 hovered in the high 30s and low 40s. In the 2000s, it rose steadily but slowly, through the mid-40s. In 2018, 49.8 percent of all trips to the plate began 0-1. That, as much as anything, captures in microcosm the nature of hitting in MLB today.

A countdown clock toward strike three begins ticking almost the moment a batter takes his place in the box. The league's adjusted OPS+ on the first pitch was higher in 2018 than ever before, and that has been true in most of the last 10 seasons. Batters hit .264/.289/.442 in all plate appearances in which they swung at the first pitch last season, and .241/.330/.395 in all plate appearances in which they took that first offering.

The percentage differences in batting average and isolated power there favor swinging at the first pitch by more than in any season since 1988, while the difference in on-base percentage favors taking by more than ever. If you want to get on base at a decent clip, it's a good idea to be patient, but you run the risk of missing the only chances you'll get to produce power.

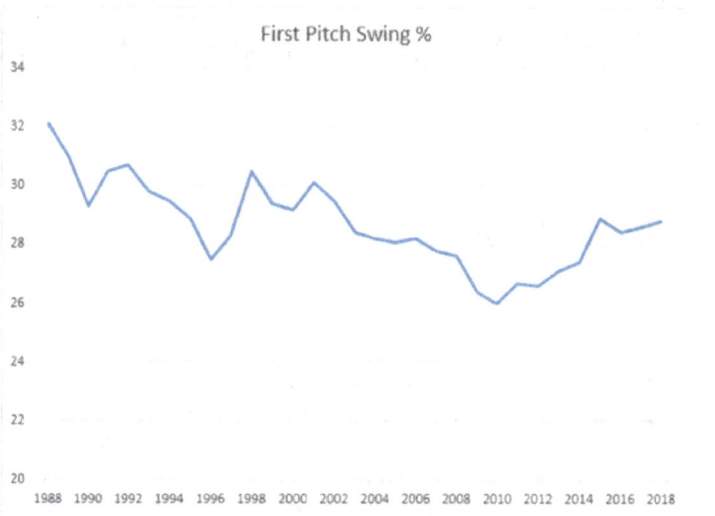

The league swung at the first pitch 28.8 percent of the time in 2018. With the isolated exception of 2015, that's the highest that number has climbed since 2002, but it might not be high enough. With the help of BP research maven Rob McQuown, I looked at the aggregate Called Strike Probability (CSProb) on the first pitch for each season since 2008, when the implementation of PITCHf/x first made measuring that possible. It's risen sharply during that period.

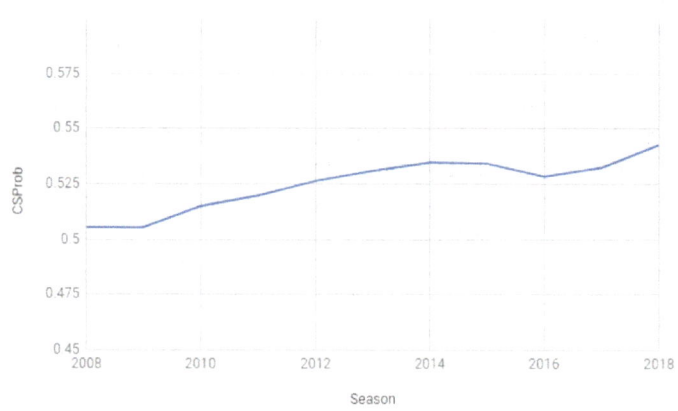

Called Strike Probability, First Pitch of PA (2008-2018)

Called Strike Probability is exactly what it sounds like: a pitch with a given CSProb has roughly that chance of being called a strike, if not swung at. In 2018, a batter who took 100 first pitches from a random sampling of the league's pitchers might expect to fall behind 54 or 55 times—up from 50 or 51 times in 2008. Almost regardless of pitch type (and, notably, especially in the case of fastballs), the first pitch tends to have more of the zone right now than ever before.

Pitchers are better at throwing strikes. They have better stuff, and believe more in their ability to miss bats within the zone. Perhaps most importantly, they know that batters are looking for one thing on the first pitch: a fastball. If they don't get it, they're likely to take the pitch. Check out how the use of sinkers and four-seamers on the first pitch has changed in a decade:

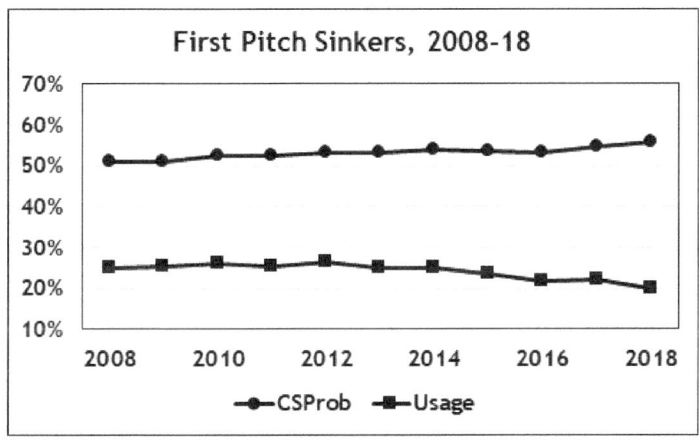

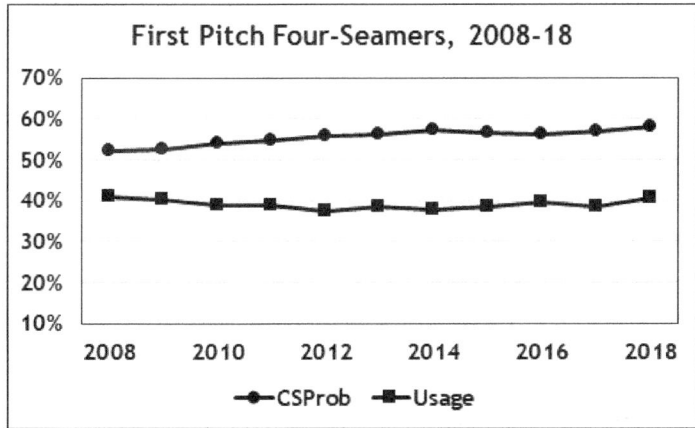

The sinker is losing its place in baseball, but the rate at which pitchers have thrown it on the first pitch hasn't dropped any faster than its usage rate in other counts. Pitchers have actually gone to their four-seamer *more* often to open counts, in the last few years, after a dip in the 2012-2015 period. What's really changed, though, and what shows up in both charts above, is that pitchers are catching more of the zone with first-pitch fastballs than they were a decade ago, or a half-decade ago. They're attacking right away, even with the pitch they know batters are expecting. The message is pretty clear: batters are being too passive.

Sliders, curves, and changeups each have more of the zone when thrown on the first pitch than they did several years ago, too, though the effect is less pronounced. Pitchers have seen the numbers; they know batters are doing better on the first pitch itself. They still feel safe throwing more and better strikes than ever before, figuring they'll come out ahead as long as they keep getting ahead to open each battle.

The Moneyball revolution brought an increased league-wide focus on OBP, which resulted in a de facto mandate to take a more patient tack at the plate. It worked very well for a while, as batters with poor plate discipline were compelled to either adjust or be expelled from the league, and pitchers with poor control were slowly weeded out.

However, concurrent with that revolution, and spurred by it in some ways, was the evolution of the pitching paradigm that now dominates the game. As batters ratcheted up their focus on inflating pitch counts and working walks, pitchers honed theirs on throwing strikes and missing bats. The league's understanding of what makes a good pitcher improved at least as much, from the mid-1990s through the mid-2000s, as its understanding of what makes a good hitter. As amphetamines and other performance-enhancing drugs were phased mostly out of the game, and as PITCHf/x broke onto the scene, individuals and teams learned how to exploit the evolved approaches of even the smartest hitters.

The ability to avoid making outs is still the most valuable one in baseball, but the magnitude of its eclipse of slugging is smaller than ever. To a greater extent than power, on-base skills derive their value from chaining—from the on-base skill levels of the players on either side of a given individual. Eleven years ago, when the housing crisis hit, people learned the hard way that the value of their homes depended a good deal on the values of their neighbors' homes. The same wasn't true, though, of their cars. So it is now, with OBP and SLG.

The global OBP in 2018 was .318. The only seasons since the Dead Ball Era in which the league got on base at a worse clip were 2013-2015, 1988, 1971-1972, and 1963-1968. This is all happening despite the aforementioned evolution of the science of hitting. It's happening despite a shift in approach and focus, one that would steer OBP ever higher, if only it were working.

Instead, it's sitting at a low ebb, and while it does so, even guys who get on base often are a little less helpful than they were 10 years ago—or 20, or 40, or 60, or 70, or 80, or 90. They're less helpful, that is, because unless there happen to be three or four other guys in the lineup who get on just as regularly, their contribution is merely to forestall the inevitable. Runs happen, increasingly, when a sudden bang happens, and that means attacking early in the count—because pitchers are sure as hell doing that.

In a league making contact on barely 75 percent of its swings, and a league in which an increasing number of pitchers can throw multiple off-speed pitches for strikes in any count, the only way to consistently generate offense is going to be aggressive. This isn't necessarily true for individuals, like Mookie Betts and Jose Ramirez, who make a lot of contact and have excellent plate discipline, and whose power comes from such natural quickness in a short stroke. Most players have to make tradeoffs, though, whether it be lowering their contact rate or raising their chase rate, in order to consistently make the quality of contact necessary to survive in today's game.

Highest %	Lowest %
Javier Baez – 48.3	Joe Mauer – 4.6
Freddie Freeman – 47.1	Mookie Betts – 9.7
Ozzie Albies – 46.3	Brett Gardner – 10.7
Jose Altuve – 44.2	Jose Ramirez – 12.0
Nick Castellanos – 44.1	Jason Kipnis – 13.8
Joey Gallo – 42.3	Jesus Aguilar – 14.5
Corey Dickerson – 40.9	Xander Bogaerts – 15.8
Salvador Perez – 40.8	Brian Dozier – 16.3
Eddie Rosario – 40.7	Mike Trout – 17.6
Nick Ahmed – 40.4	Yasmani Grandal – 17.6

Top 10 and Bottom 10 Hitters, First-Pitch Swing Rate (2018)

The question isn't which of these lists one prefers, but what they each convey, qualitatively, about the cat-and-mouse game of early-count hitting. Those top five on the left, especially, drive home the fact that for most players, getting aggressive early in the count is now key to keeping strikeout rate down and hitting for power.

For now, the message is: pitchers are coming right after batters with the nastiest stuff they've ever had. Batters had better stop giving away strike one and force hurlers to adjust, or the global OBP crisis is only going to get worse.

—*Matthew Trueblood is an author of Baseball Prospectus.*

A Hymn for the Index Stat

Patrick Dubuque

We survived without computers. I know this, because I remember the day when my dad hooked up his brand-new Atari 400 computer to the back of our 12-inch Magnavox television, and the perfect blue of the memo pad lit up for the first time. I was born just on the edge of that transitional generation, of learning cursive and balancing checkbooks and just doing math all the time, constant manual arithmetic.

It still amazes me. We learned how to sail ships without computers. We learned how to do calculus. We built towers that didn't fall down, most of the time. We engineered catapults to knock them down anyway. We built a robust system of philosophy called "utilitarianism," founded on the principle that the good of an action is evaluated by summing the effects of that action, which is the kind of formula that would make the world's mainframes crash. The whole foundation of statistics as a field is "here's math you could easily do but would die of old age first."

The fact of the matter is that there is too much math in the world to do. There are too many things changing, and too many things too small to notice, for us to handle. At some point, they become too much for the computers to handle as well, which is why we have chaos theory and undetectable earthquakes, but it's not an even fight. At some point, we fall back on intuition, and given how under-equipped we are, we're forced to bestow that intuition with some sort of supernatural superiority, the "gut feeling," that we can't prove because we can only intuit that our intuition is better.

We're all lousy at intuition, and wonderful at lying to ourselves about it. The honest truth is that computers are far better at intuition than we are, because in order to know what feels "off" you have to know what's "on." In order to do that you have to constantly reassess the average of everything, then re-rank your own experience against it.

Test your own, by comparing these three anonymous lines:

Player	G	HR	AVG	OBP	SLG
Player A	156	38	.259	.342	.535
Player B	154	38	.280	.348	.527
Player C	158	38	.266	.343	.509

These all seem like pretty similar players, right? The second one a touch more batted-ball dependent, the third a little less strong, but all pretty good hitters. And you'd be right, about the latter. Not the former.

Here's the breakdown:

- Player A: 1991 Howard Johnson, 141 DRC+
- Player B: 1996 Dean Palmer, 121 DRC+
- Player C: 2018 Giancarlo Stanton, 114 DRC+

Baseball is fortunate to have escaped the seismic shifts of so many other sports, where the talents and performances of other eras are nearly unrecognizable. (And not just other sports: try to explain the greatness of the movie Duck Soup without adjusting for era.) But they're still there, and they're nearly impossible to account for manually, without having to resort to sweeping generalizations like "steroid era" or juiced-ball era" to throw out entire swathes of production.

This is all to say that we should celebrate the index stat, that simple 100-based scale with such a humble aim: just to give context. It's hard to imagine how we lived without them for so long. Sabermetricians have always tried to make their stats look like other stats: True Average mapped to batting average, FIP molded to look like and compare to ERA. It's easy to understand the motivation—these statistics carry an emotional value in them that is hard to resist, as with the .300 hitter and the 2.00 ERA—but even they fall prey to the same loss of scale as their unadjusted counterparts. If a .300 average means different things in different years, does that hold true for a .300 True Average?

Instead, 100 doesn't say anything, except above average or below. And it does it instantly, for every season in every run environment for any statistic we want it to. We should have more index stats: K%+, so we can stop comparing Mike Clevinger's career 9.46 K/9 to Nolan Ryan's 9.55. HBP%+, so we can note that Ron Hunt was getting plunked when nobody else was getting plunked, as opposed to that imitator Brandon Guyer. Some might note how stale these references are and accuse league-adjustment as a backward-looking drive, and this is true. But we're always looking backward, always comparing the new with the expectations already set. The index stat just forces us to be honest.

There's always resistance to a new statistic, especially one so outwardly simple and so internally complex. We tend to stick with what we know, even in the case of formulas that are supposed to tell us what we know. But if your resistance is that it seems too complicated, too counterintuitive, too "black boxy," I encourage you to consider why you feel that way. Because the real world is infinitely more complicated than baseball, where all the pitches go in one basic direction and the baserunners are only allowed to travel in four directions. Baseball statistics based on mixed methodology are almost impossibly intricate. So are skyscrapers and automobiles. That's why we have computers—to take the guesswork out of them.

—*Patrick Dubuque is an author of Baseball Prospectus.*

Index of Names

Allen, Nick	88, 99	Joseph, Corban	88
Anderson, Brett	46	Kaprielian, James	97
Anderson, Tanner	89	Kiekhefer, Dean	89
Armenteros, Lazaro	80, 95	Laureano, Ramon	34
Barreto, Franklin	20	Luzardo, Jesus	86, 91
Bassitt, Chris	48	Manaea, Sean	62
Beck, Austin	81, 95	Mateo, Jorge	82, 97
Blackburn, Paul	89	Mengden, Daniel	64
Blevins, Jerry	50	Merrell, Kevin	88, 99
Bridwell, Parker	89	Montas, Frankie	66
Brooks, Aaron	89	Murphy, Sean	83, 92
Buchter, Ryan	52	Murray, Kyler	93
Canha, Mark	22	Neuse, Sheldon	84
Chapman, Matt	24	Olson, Matt	36
Davis, Khris	26	Pennington, Cliff	88
Deichmann, Greg	88, 100	Petit, Yusmeiro	68
Dull, Ryan	89	Phegley, Josh	88
Dunshee, Parker	89	Pinder, Chad	38
Eierman, Jeremy	88, 100	Piscotty, Stephen	40
Estrada, Marco	54	Profar, Jurickson	42
Feigl, Brady	89	Puk, A.J.	87, 92
Fiers, Mike	56	Ramirez, Tyler	88
Fowler, Dustin	28	Rodney, Fernando	70
Gossett, Daniel	58	Semien, Marcus	44
Grossman, Robbie	30	Soria, Joakim	72
Hannah, Jameson	88, 98	Taylor, Beau	88
Hendriks, Liam	60	Treinen, Blake	74
Herrmann, Chris	88	Triggs, Andrew	76
Holmes, Grant	85, 96	Trivino, Lou	78
Hundley, Nick	32	Wendelken, J.B.	89
Jefferies, Daulton	100		

Ballpark diagrams for Baseball Prospectus are created by THIRTY81Project, a design concept offering original ballpark artwork, including the new 'Ballparks of 2019' 11 x 17 color print.

Visit **www.thirty81project.com** for full details.